Get Connected

Making the Right Connections

Get Connected
Making the Right Connections

ELEAZAR ANTHONY NOEL

GET CONNECTED
Marking the Right Connections

Published by Ibusol Limited
Copyright © 2017 by Eleazar Anthony Noel
Cover design by Roland Ali Pantin
Interior design by Digital Innovation Designs

First Printing: December 2017

ISBN 978-1-387-29824-2

www.eleazarnoel.com

DEDICATION

This is for you dad!

Contents

Acknowledgements

I would not be the person I am today without the blessing of having been surrounded by some incredible people. I was born into a family that molded me to be the best that I could possibly be and I, in turn, have adopted a family that helped me grow by seeing the best in me. I am forever grateful for both my biological and spiritual family.

I feel like I am at the center of a web, connected to individuals who are connected to other individuals, who in turn are connected to businesses and other professionals. Being at the center of this web has taught me many things, one of which is that some connections last for a moment and some for a lifetime. Regardless of how long they last, these connections have brought me to this point in my life. What is the point of having such connections? We humans are social beings, we cannot do everything alone, and such connections work in our favor if we make good use of them. The journey to this point of completing my first book could not have been possible without the guidance, love, support and patience of some very special individuals in my life.

Firstly, I would like to acknowledge the Creator who before anyone else believed in me, inspired me and stood by me through it all, and still stands by me.

To my father, Clyde Noel, the simple lessons you taught me when I was a child continue to inspire me to this day. To my aunt, Ann Marie Noel – Samaroo, you played the role of mother, sister, friend, teacher, manager, and my advisor. I have so much to thank you for. My cousin Darrel Noel, your determination to become a better person continues to inspire me to do the same.

To my brothers and sisters—Irijah Noel, Elijah Noel, Eleashar Noel, Dario Alibin, Christian Felipe Fernandez Espinosa, Sarah Noel, Daphne Noel, Rebekah Beckles, Rachel Beckles—you have all added so much value to my personal and professional life, THANK YOU, THANK YOU, THANK YOU. Extra special thanks to Kimberly Mullen, my big sister; your love, your friendship, and your guidance is a direct blessing from the Creator.

My many nephews and nieces all around the world, Keyunta, Jeylin, Elijah, Irijah, Kareem, Akilah, Isaiah, Seker, Heru, Ezekiel, Michaiah, Zaccai, just to name a few, thank you all for reminding me that the best way to teach is by example.

To my lifelong friends who make up part of my extended family, Sandy Smith, Feola Jerome, Fane Strachan, Inka Williams, Kwasi Gill, Nicole Rajnauth, Dale Enoch, John-Michael Mader, Jo-anne Pierre, Sandra Basheer and Elisha Le Maitre, thank you all for supporting my journey.

To my team of consultants and personal advisors, the wisdom and knowledge you all passed onto me over the years have truly help to shape me. Your professionalism, analytical thinking, constructive criticism and ability to step out of the box and look in have helped me in many ways.

To my past teachers and lecturers, especially Mrs. Ramdoo, Mrs. Frank Felix, Ms. Lynatte Francis, I am forever grateful for the foundation you have helped to create. Thank you all for imparting your knowledge unto me.

I am grateful for the ever-growing network of incredible people I have met from around the world who have continued to support me and my many projects.

THANK YOU ALL!!!

Foreword

Networking is an essential skill, and if done right, it can certainly be one of the most rewarding personal skills for any professional. I have learned this over my twenty plus years as a professional dance artist and cultural ethnologist.

A born businessman and entrepreneur—Eleazar Anthony Noel has been refining the skillful art of business and networking from since he was a young boy. I had the pleasure of meeting Eleazar when he was 11 years old while I resided on the island of Tobago conducting post-graduate cultural studies research. At this young age, he was managing his family's successful artisan business at a bustling market place that attracted a diverse range of people from different cultures and countries from all over the world. I was impressed with his natural ability to not only command his business but to do it in such a likable and personable manner. People were magnetized by him and the business was successful because of that.

From an early age, he learned the value of connecting to others and the meaning of building relationships as the first ingredients towards creating a successful business. Looking back on the trajectory of his life's accomplishments over the past 20 years, I can equate his professional successes to a lifetime of mastering the business of inter-relating to people. These early formative years, he experienced first hand the key to a successful business begins with the ability to establish meaningful relationships with others.

Over the past 20 years that we have remained in contact, he has evolved into a global leader and visionary in his field with his international corporation, ELE Training & Consulting Services. Through lectures, books, events, and training, Eleazar inspires rising entrepreneurs to form the right connections for business growth. In his everyday life, he reminds us of our basic human need and desire for people to make meaningful "connections" in their lives.

Kimberly Miguel Mullen
www.kimberlymiguelmullen.com

Introduction

In the business world, there's nothing truer than the adage: "It's not what you know, it's who you know." When seeking employment, it can mean helping you get the job you want, as employers sift through hundreds, even thousands, of applications. A good word from a friend can help pull your application from the slush pile and put you on top, if not get you the job outright. The simple and, these days, often-forgotten fact is that knowing the right people can get you to the right place faster than any other way.

We've come a long way from the times when the only way to do business was by word of mouth. If you were a baker, you made bread. Eventually, everyone in your village knew, and if the bread was good, they came. Not a thought was given to having a networking plan. Networking has evolved throughout the centuries so much that as recently as a few decades ago, college kids could seek out what pub their professor favored and spend their nights developing a relationship with them, and in doing so, not only would they probably enhance your interest for the subject he or she taught, but they would gain free knowledge that wasn't shared in class. Today, having drinks with a professor would be frowned upon, but there are still ways to develop relationships with influential people and make connections with professionals. Fraternities, academic clubs, high-profile schools, all have the same thing in common, in that they're geared at bringing select like-minded people together.

Networking has been a secret thread connecting successful people throughout time, and if you feel that by not knowing the "right people" you might be at a disadvantage, you might be surprised to learn that networking creates success on many different levels. Meeting people is important, but it is also important to know how to conduct yourself, and what to do to make simply meeting people successful business networking.

In Get Connected: Making the Right Connections, you'll find new ways to expand your social outreach and learn how stepping across into new markets will help open opportunities for you. Whether you're a small business owner, or an individual looking to get ahead, learn how to grow your network in a way that will make it work for you. Without the right tools, you'd be surprised how difficult it can be to network, but fear not, you will soon be one step closer to helping ensure your success today. With this book, you'll gain knowledge and tools that, unlike much of the business-related information we learn today, will be useful for the future to come.

The Essentials of Networking

Every business, every position, has one thing in common: a job cannot be done without using some form of communication. Communicating with others is something we do every day, but to a greater extent, communicating clearly and making lasting impressions are skills that require good perception and talent. Essentially, networking is a form of communication, and the correlation is that the greater the communication, the greater the outreach, and as a result, the more successful a business tends to be.

Networking Can Make or Break a Business

Business owners know all too well the wide range of elements typically used in order to measure whether or not their businesses are successful. Large companies can easily spend millions of dollars in advertising and marketing with hopes of reaching customers. For smaller businesses, however, if a marketing budget is available at all, it's usually too small to compete with the big hitters and is often dependent upon whatever free tools are available online. Nonetheless, even well budgeted marketing campaigns will hit snags as, with time, those same marketing dollars reach fewer and fewer people and companies cannibalize themselves by resorting to stealing customers from each other.

Throughout history, businesses have relied on networking in order to grow, and even currently, several unique companies exist that rely strictly on networking for their business growth. Take, for example, The Girl Scouts of the United States of America (GSUSA), more commonly referred to as The Girl Scouts. Their secret for selling cookies each year, the gross source of income for the program, lies within their network. They offer no marketing, no commercials, and no coupons; they rely simply on friends and family to help them sell cookies. Does it matter if they have everyone in their family helping out? No. What matters instead is *who* is helping out; it's those friends and family members who know people interested in buying cookies. The whole process is simple enough, but the email sent to you by a coworker whose granddaughter is a girl scout—the one letting you know that cookies will be available soon—works because of the relationship that person has with you. If the coworker is pleasant, has established a good relationship with you, and appears to be willing to help you when you need it, chances are, you're willing to buy the cookies. Sure, they're good cookies, but knowing you're helping out can make a big difference and can even serve as the deciding factor in making the purchase.

Relationships have been the basis of business transactions for years, and although business models change, products change, and companies change, one thing many successful companies have today is their ability to create and maintain good relationships with their customers. Maintaining good relationships ties into communications, which in turn is the essence of networking. Although typical networking is usually perceived as socializing, companies have to develop good relationships with their customers as well. We describe this form of communication as having good customer service. Networking tends to be a system in which both parties benefit from the relationship, but once you understand that good communication is the foundation of networking, it will make understanding the process easier.

Bad Communication

It may sound simple so far, but don't take your ability to clearly communicate for granted. You may understand how good communication can help a business succeed, but it's just as important to look at companies that have had trouble because of poor communication, or companies that could have used good communication to prevent or deter their demise. Recently Subway, a sandwich chain with locations around the world, which in recent years had been one of the fastest growing fast-food chains around, hit a roadblock as the result of some bad publicity. It began on the internet, as things so often do these days, when a story emerged of a customer who measured their sandwich and posted on social media that their 'foot long' sandwich was in reality only 11 inches long. Subway's response was not an apology. Instead, they explained that the term 'foot long' was meant to be a name for the sandwich, a registered trademark, and not meant to be used as a form of measurement for their sandwiches. This caused a wave of bad reviews and angry customers, who claimed deceit. Now, the company might not have been trying to be deceitful, but if nothing else, they failed at communicating with their customers. Even if their sandwiches were not intended to be 12 inches long, calling them 'foot long' was a clear representation of intended size. For Subway, stating later that the term 'foot long' meant something other than its literal meaning was poor communication, which will eventually lead a company to fail. Little was done afterward to try and repair the incident or to make amends with angry customers, and because Subway failed to maintain a good relationship with the people who ate there, sales declined.

This is only one example of how poor communication was bad for business, but the same goes for anyone: communicating clearly and honestly will help build relationships, and this, in turn, is the essence of networking.

Honesty Pays Off

As a child growing up, there are steady reminders that reiterate the importance of being honest. As adults, there's no one there to scold you when you're not telling the truth, but being honest is important at any age, not just as children. There's a good reason why parents instill this trait into their progeny; because honesty plays an important role throughout a lifetime. For some, growing up garners a different set of rules, and with no one watching, it's easy to meander away from moral teachings.

Pick up a newspaper, and it would be no surprise to find that another company is in hot water for not being honest. In today's corporate climate, companies are too busy focusing on profits and managers are too worried about hitting sales forecast numbers that a trade-off is made in which veracity takes a back seat to profitability. Think of how many dishonest business people you come across in just one day. Did a representative from the cable company call and promise you a great deal, only to have you misled into paying more than you thought you would? Did you receive an email asking for sensitive information from a long lost family descendant in Kenya, knowing your family lineage came from somewhere else? How about the purchase you made online, and the product never arrived, or the one you were shipped was a cheap, inferior copy of what you were expecting?

As for Subway, the company responded in a way that made it appear dishonest about the products it was selling. Remember, Subway admitted that they didn't intend their sandwiches to be a particular length; they simply called it a 'foot long'. Sure, they could call their sandwich anything they'd like, but in the opinions of many, they believed they were buying a 12 inch-long sandwich. Perhaps it's difficult to control the actual size of the bread once it's being baked—another explanation that was given later—but Subway was thought to be selling sandwiches of a particular length.

Had the company simply apologized and recognized that it had made a mistake, the outcome could have been different. Companies around the world go through these types of challenges all the time. To some, it's almost expected that there would be a catch of some sort, somewhere in the fine print and that the company you're dealing with is only out to get your money.

Honesty is therefore crucial in the business world. Aside from just being good morals, there's an unseen formula that develops naturally when a person practices fairness. What tends to occur is that when a person has another person's trust—businesses included—a higher level of confidence is typically achieved, and this confidence in a person's actions or intentions is valuable for building or maintaining relationships. This explains why you were willing to buy Girl Scout cookies from your kind coworker, or why you stopped going to Subway. When there's confidence, there also tends to be commitment, and these are all parts of the working elements of networking.

It's important to first understand the essentials of networking, as they set the tone for building relationships with others. Communicating clearly requires a little bit of strategy, as you learn to understand and even anticipate the needs of others. Honesty is important, for several reasons, and while you understand the breakdown of why it's important, in reality, it should require little consideration; it should instead have been made into part of your persona. If nothing more than for your peace of mind, know that being honest will keep things simpler, as Mark Twain famously said, "If you tell the truth, you don't have to remember anything."

Understanding Networking

Not Just Meeting People

Much of what we understand networking to be is wrong. Sure, the term is used widely, and we hear it and use it on a regular basis, but true networking takes time to master. However, after reading *Get Connected: Making the Right Connections* you will have a great advantage over most, and you'll be years ahead of the game. When asked "What is networking?" many people simply reply, "Meeting people," but when asked *how* you meet people, the response is usually followed by a long pause.

Networking by definition is an extended group of people with comparable interests or concerns who interact for mutual assistance or support. Now, let's look at what that actually means. Typical networking occurs in many different ways. Companies can have trade shows where several vendors attend to meet and offer their products. Organizations can have workshops in which people come to learn something about a particular product or idea. Car companies have car shows where the newest models are revealed, giving journalists and car enthusiasts a chance to help promote their products. Companies can have meetings with other companies so that one can teach the other about new products or new techniques of doing something within a particular line of business. By all means, these are great ways of meeting new people and should be seen as opportunities to grow your networking web, but these are just a few examples of how networking occurs. Within all these examples described, the sole purpose for meeting others is—as the definition implies—to interact; however, I would like to tweak the definition a little. Instead of saying 'for mutual assistance' we'll say 'to *offer assistance*', and this will help shed some light on our understanding of networking.

Focus Less on Yourself

As human beings, when meeting others, we generally tend to focus on ourselves, but with good intentions. We want others to like us, and find us interesting, or recognize us for our talents and abilities. However, it's critical that you understand that networking should be, for the most part, an outer experience. Often, especially with young entrepreneurs, there's an innate state-of-mind of wanting something or of wanting to be part of a deal only after it's clear the outcome will prove to be evidently beneficial to them. If you're not already an altruistic person, know that putting yourself first doesn't necessarily make you a selfish person, not in the sense of networking. What you're trying to prove to someone when you're networking with them is that you're worthy of their time by proving that you are worth interacting with, and by extension, worthy of their business.

Networking is reciprocal, and once you realize that networking is a two-way street, where the rewards come afterward as a result of making connections for the future, you begin to understand the importance of putting others over yourself. No longer will you have to worry about what others think of you if you simply project yourself as being strong and confident, but more so, present yourself as someone who is willing to help others. In chapter one, we discussed how honesty is an essential element of networking. Now that you know it's in your best interest to be honest, you will have a similar affect on people in that you'll appear to be a warm and trustworthy person, and this, by far, will make a better first impression than anything else.

Have Something to Give

Networking, meeting others, making good impressions, and building lasting relationships are made possible by having something to offer to others. If you worry about what's in it for you, you will not be able to make the types of connections that may be of value to you later. Instead, give first, and watch the two-way street of networking work for you, as others give back. Once you've built the network with confidence, knowing what you have to offer others will come to you naturally, but in the meantime, there is something you have that is of great value to others. One of the greatest things you can share with others is information, and you'd be surprised by how much interesting information you have to share with others. Having good information to share doesn't require having gone to the best schools, or being a "know-it-all", but there are things you know that are unique to your own life experiences and knowledge that you can share with others. Sometimes, the best anecdotal advice comes from stories about relatives, or funny experiences you had. If nothing else, offer your honest opinion about the topic or recommend a book you read, or a website you tried; perhaps an article you read in a magazine or newspaper can help you present yourself as someone with something to offer. A great way to expand your network would be to give someone a valuable introduction, or offer a referral, or recommend the new person to someone you might already know. Your ability to help others will be clearly presented to others when you have something to give.

Practice Being a Good Listener

We understand that when meeting others, people tend to want to focus on themselves and, aside from being a distraction by keeping you from focusing on others, it also makes listening difficult as well. When offering to help others, strike a balance between *giving* and *receiving.* A person may choose not to listen to others for many reasons. Some reasons are simply out of the person's control, whether they find the other person interesting or not, or have feelings of anxiety, which can make it difficult to focus on someone else. Those who prefer talking to listening are sometimes known as 'controlling listeners'—they are people who feel the need to talk about themselves and refer often to their personal experiences. Another type of listener is a 'passive listener', who often has no trouble listening, as they feel it involves no special talent to perform, and can just sit back and let the conversation happen. A good conversation, however, usually requires a good balance of listening and speaking, and requires the listener to actively participate with the person speaking. When actively listening, make yourself a mental outline of what the person speaking is doing. Some things to focus on are:

- Predict what will come next;
- Relate their points to your experiences;
- Look for similarities and differences;
- Ask questions.

These are things you may be doing when meeting someone new, someone you want to network with or someone you want to add to your group of networkers. Show the person that they have your attention by making eye contact periodically. Staring may be considered offensive to some, or in some cultures, but use making eye contact as a tool, which make both people comfortable when done appropriately. Be attentive to the person's behavior during the interaction. A person's behavior may be a key indicator as to what type of questions to ask, or serve as a cue for when to offer your feedback. Be patient, and let the person finish speaking before asking questions. When you do ask questions, ensure that your tone is friendly and non-threatening, so that you are perceived as having good intentions. When you're not sure what types of questions to ask, restate or summarize what the person said; this is an effective tool for interacting with the speaker. Another thing to consider when interacting with others is to try to show empathy by demonstrating that you care about the subject, and are willing to listen; however, don't criticize or express yourself in a judgmental fashion. Remember, you want to earn the person's trust and confidence, and this could be easily lost by engaging with a bad attitude, or by giving poor advice.

Meeting Someone New

Do:
- Make eye contact;
- Be attentive to their behavior;
- Be patient, and wait before speaking;
- Interact, offer advice or ask questions;
- Show empathy.

Don't:
- Make things about 'me';
- Be a passive listener;
- Be a 'controlling listener';
- Criticize;
- Be negative.

Knowing is Half the Battle

If anyone can remember the slogan, "Knowing is half the battle," then you're probably in your late twenties or early thirties or older. In the early eighties, the original GI Joe cartoon showed a group of rogue warriors out to fight the evil Cobra members. At the end of each show, a child, or group of children, would appear and reveal the moral of the show, to which the child would say ". . . and now I know," and GI Joe would reply, "And knowing is half the battle."

This slogan couldn't be more true when learning about the person you're speaking with. If part of what you're trying to capture when meeting someone is capturing their attention, showing genuine mutual respect, and an interest in what the person has to say, then it would pay you handsomely to try and learn what you can about the person you would be speaking to, whenever possible, so that you can better connect with them.

You can find out a lot about a person, especially another professional, by simply finding their Facebook or LinkedIn profile. Knowing specific details about a person's job or position can open up great opportunities for carrying on a conversation with them. The more you're able to relate to someone, the better your ability to communicate, and this then enhances the possibility of establishing a good relationship with them. If you do find something out about the person whom you're attempting to network with, use it to your advantage as you might find it easy to congratulate them on their new position, or praise them for a recognition they may have received.

When attending a networking event, it is a good idea to know beforehand who will be there, what industries will be involved, or even what level of business professionals you might encounter. There is no guarantee that with the right planning, the right mentality, and meeting the right people will create a vast network for anyone. Networking takes time, and it requires meeting lots of people who are willing to help you. However, if you're honest, and have a sense of wanting to help others, and follow the few steps you've been taught so far, you'll greatly improve your networking situation. Keep in mind that the person you are meeting is investing their time by meeting you, and they deserve your full attention. Be sincere, and show some interest in what they have to say, as people in general know when someone is not being genuine. A person who speaks without listening, who appears to be in a hurry, and goes around handing out their business card without being asked for it, is in no way networking with others. For the most part, know that when you're networking, the people speaking to each other are simply getting to know each other, so tell them about yourself or about your company, and make sure to show them you have something to offer; whether that's information, or by making a referral, but one thing you don't want to do is to be quick to try and sign them up, or sell them on a product. Doing so will make you come off as desperate, and you don't ever want to be seen as being desperate. Instead, warming up to someone, seeing how the two of you can help each other, is what the intended goal should be. Once the potential for a relationship has been established, the next step would be to offer to stay connected, but we'll cover that in a later chapter.

Why Should I Get Connected

Why is Networking so Important?

Networking is not something you learned about in school, even for some business majors—they merely touch on the topic briefly—and it's not something mom and dad pulled you aside and explained to you in detail, but given how vital networking is for success, it's a mystery why more people are not spreading the word. At this point, you understand the essence of networking, and how it's more than just meeting people, but do you understand how important it is to your success? Imagine you're new to a company, and you're confident about yourself; you're intelligent, you have a good appearance, you're polite and eager to make a name for yourself at your first real job. Your boss speaks with you and hands over an assignment she thinks you can take on. Since you understand the importance of networking, you seek out help from others, make some new contacts in different departments—people you'll be able to contact when assigned future projects—and you finish your project without a hiccup, letting your boss know that she was right in trusting the assignment to you.

At the same time you were hired, another person came on as well, but they work for a different department and you haven't had the chance to meet with them quite yet. Now, imagine that this other employee was also assigned a task that was similar in nature to yours. Your fellow employee is your age, he dresses nicely, and his educational level is similar to yours, but where the two of you differ is that he, unfortunately, doesn't understand the value of networking. Being new to the company, the other employee tries to take on the project alone and makes several mistakes along the way. Despite using his best judgment, he gets major aspects of the project wrong. After a day or so, his boss then decides to assign the project to a more senior employee—not to punish him, but because that assignment might have been a prerequisite for another project that will follow and needs to be successfully completed within a particular time frame.

Even from day one, understanding the importance of building your network, starting with internal contacts, helped you understand who to go to for help, and opened up doors for you to establish relationships with those whom you may benefit from, but also, those who may benefit from you. This is only one example of how networking helped elevate your status with the boss, and this is without even having the chance to have established a closer, professional relationship with her first. Imagine, how many other opportunities can networking offer?

Opportunities Created by Networking

There are many correlations between good leaders and those who successfully network. To some, it can appear to be hard work, and many people even dread having to reach out to people and form relationships with them. The way some people see it, looking at a leader or manager from a non-managers' point of view, is that the person they are seeing is instead being manipulative, using others for the sole purpose of benefitting themselves. This is typically not true, but the similarities are that good leaders know where to find the help they need, just like those with strong networking skills.

A person with a strong network understands that their relationships with others will help provide important feedback, insight, and information that will help when making important decisions. In the example above of how networking will help you even when first starting a new job, you could see how big of a difference it made knowing where to go for help, and establishing contacts along the way. Building good relationships with people within your immediate surroundings is a form of internal networking. Internal networking benefits everyone as employees seek the help of other employees, and allows everyone to perform more efficiently. Instead of trying to take on large tasks head-on, seeking help from others can help make long assignments easier to manage. Relying on the talents of others to perform a specialized task can benefit a person who could otherwise invest their time on something else. For the most part, internal networking is oriented toward current demands and relies on a company to have an organized structure, where you not only receive help from others but can contribute to the needs of others as well. Within internal networking, the number of persons involved can include a wide range of people from both sides of the corporate ladder.

A large part of why a person becomes interested in networking is to enhance their personal or professional development, and this is where external networking works best at creating new opportunities. Look at external networking as a way of building relationships with those outside your inner circle of friends and co-workers. These are the persons you would meet through professional associates, alumni groups, clubs and other places of common interest, in which these *outside* people can provide a potential means of enhancing your career or business. The basis of networking is to establish relationships, and while it may not appear that anyone in your network is enhancing your career or business directly, many times, the people in your external network will provide important referrals, or relay information to you from other contacts, and they can often serve by way of developmental support such as coaching or mentoring. Build strong relationships with the people in your external network as these are the people you would rely on to invite you to social events and gatherings.

When invited, remember to ask who else will be there, and research these people when possible so that by being prepared you can initiate conversations with potential contacts and further expand your network. What makes external networking so valuable is essentially the potential for referral opportunities. While internal networking is a good first step to networking, over time, professionals tend to shift their focus from internal networking to external networking. But having a good mixture of both at the beginning is essential for both short-term and long-term business goals.

Business Networks

In the past, a company or business would view others in the same industry as the so-called competition and would avoid collaborating with them out of spite or territorialism. But someone who knows the value of networking knows that bad business relationships, even with so-called competition in the same industry, can be detrimental for business in general.

Consider for a moment, a person with a small business, who like many small businesses, struggle to earn new clients and establish a strong foot-hold within their industry. By reaching out and building relationships with people in similar positions or similar companies to yours, others will contribute to your knowledge and they could even share information about their clients' needs, helping to generate ideas and ways of developing the services you'd need for your customers. For the small business owner, networking might seem like a backwards way of thinking, or could even be seen as not conducive to a growing business as the main factor, time, is already limited. In contrast, by networking with other businesses a company can spend less time finding new ways of tackling problems, as a sharing of best practices provides valuable information that can be used to work more efficiently. For a large company, spending lots of time and money on a project to help improve a particular aspect of a company is quite common, even when the outcome might not prove to be beneficial in the end. The concept is similar to the idea of learning from the mistakes of others—in business networking, the sharing of information helps facilitate internal work tasks and individuals can avoid doing the same tasks repeatedly. Overall, business networks payoff includes helping a business find its strategic direction and organizational goals. The same way learning from others who have been successful will help you become more confident, successful networking will help people feel more engaged in their jobs. Trying to find the right people to network may at times seem like a challenge. You will learn more about how to engage the right people later in this book.

Building Relationships

Building a successful network will require some effort and creativity on your end. For many, networking is often confused with selling, "pitching" a sales offer, or an effort to try and seal the deal with someone. It's a common misconception, but know that selling has no place in networking. Networking is, instead, a systematic way of bringing people together to establish and build relationships. Learn to develop lasting relationships with a focus on the long-term perspective. Your motives for meeting others should not come from financial gain. Looking back at chapter one, remember that when meeting others, focus on the other person so that you can develop and maintain important relationships that you can later call on for your business needs.

If finding time to network seems like too much trouble and meeting people within your industry is difficult to do, focus on other aspects of yourself, such as interests outside of work, and build networking opportunities out of your extracurricular activities. Say, for example, you enjoy classical music. If once a year you could book a table at a restaurant, invite about a dozen friends, clients, or people from your external network, and go together after dinner to a live concert, you would do several things: first, everyone would have had a good time, and remember you for it; second, even if those attending were people from diverse backgrounds, and various industries, there's the potential for new contacts to be made; and third, you would have helped to solidify your relationship with these people.

Learning from others within the same industry will help you grow and learn directly from those whose experiences are similar to yours, but in the case just mentioned, where you invited people from different backgrounds and from different business sectors, a lot will be learned from each other. Hearing about their unique business problems and techniques would allow those networking together to come up with solutions that would be considered "outside-the-box" thinking. By doing something you like, where others share something in common, you take advantage of a seemingly fun situation to expand your network, cultivate relationships and build chemistry. The key to the relationship is that there is an understood mutual benefit. Once a good relationship is established, it must be maintained. Not keeping in contact with people in your network periodically will result in a loss of their support, and if a person can't come through—including yourself—at a time when the need arises, the network has failed to do its job.

More Connected Than Ever

Social networking is now more popular than ever. As of the date of publication of this book, some of the top platforms are: Facebook, with 2 billion users; Twitter, with 328 million users; LinkedIn, with 500 million; and Pinterest with 250 million users. While there are users of all ages on the social media networks, it's the younger people—those under 35—who have integrated social media into their lives thanks to the growing popularity of smartphones.

With so many social media options today—far too many to name them all—it's hard to know which one is trending, or how to find out the one that's popular with the people you'd like to network with. Predicting the future and how social media will affect networking in general is uncertain, but if one thing is certain, it's that throughout history, face-to-face networking has proven to be the best method for generating dependable contacts. If you're on Facebook, the number one social media site available today, think whether it has improved your networking abilities. Sure, it's fun to see photos of friends, and learn about new restaurants from old pals, or watch funny videos that are shared with you, but your Facebook friends still manage to be out of reach, and unless you already see them on a regular basis, true networking capabilities are out of reach due to the lack of being able to form real, personal relationships. So far, it appears that e-networking is more of grounds for content sharing than for building relationships.

Perhaps, one day, a new type of social media will emerge where participants can be more mindful at their approach to selecting who they can connect with, and serve as a tool for uniting people in person, but for now, face to face is the most successful method. Meeting someone in person has value, as it shows that you are willing to take the time to meet them, but it also allows others to recognize one of the first steps in developing a relationship with someone, which is trust. A person who can speak with you, seeing that they have your undivided attention, will trust you and perhaps want to keep you as a contact point for future reference. A personal encounter will leave a lasting impression on someone, as they look back on the night you met and remember the event, the food, the jokes —can you say that about a text or instant message?

Stepping Out of Your Comfort Zone

Become Comfortable Meeting People

For many people, the idea of speaking to complete strangers—and even worse, having to ask them for contact information—can seem quite daunting. It's understandable. After all, people grow comfortable with their circle of friends, and meeting new people is something that doesn't happen very often. If this sounds like you, and networking and reaching out to people you don't already know sounds like an unnatural act, have no fear. Even for those who are natural born extroverts, networking is a skill that must be learned.

Probably the hardest part of meeting someone is initiating the conversation. The best thing you can do to help improve your ability to feel comfortable meeting new people is to simply practice. It might feel uncomfortable at first, but by meeting new people you will become better at networking and eventually improve your communication skills. At the same time, you're likely to see the opposite effects should you choose not to practice. Networking does not always bring quick rewards, but if you stop networking because you don't see those instant rewards, it can start to feel uncomfortable meeting new people—you get out of your social groove. But if you persist, as you meet people over and over again, you will not only learn how to do it well, you will also find ways to enjoy it.

As you come to realize that networking opportunities can occur in unconventional places outside the normally expected ones such as office meetings, conventions, and other company-sponsored events, it is important to keep your behavior in line. Meeting others in places with open bars, or in places with relaxed atmospheres such as sporting events, where the general consensus is to simply relax and have fun, it can be easy to get carried away. Take into consideration that while you may be having a good time, if you're trying to make a networking connection with someone while not displaying your most professional self, you can blow your chances at making a good first impression. If that ever happens, then simply move on—there'll be other opportunities later. However, now that you're aware, you can prevent that from happening. Putting your best foot forward helps in many ways; it helps you gain the trust of others, it helps make a good first impression, it helps others to 'get' who you are, but also, it tells others that you're someone who could be considered for either a career opportunity, or to partner with, if you're a small business owner. The first impression you make is with your appearance, then with your speech, but if you're not being a professional, you're likely not unlocking potential opportunities that could be made available to you.

Ways to Explore New Opportunities

When someone hears the word "networking" they often imagine events such as job fairs, corporate dinners, and company conferences. And while these are all suitable places to make great networking connections, the truth is that there are networking opportunities everywhere.

Sporting events and concerts are great ways of rounding up a few friends and turning the event into a networking opportunity. Say, for example, you meet a friend, and a friend of theirs is someone you have taken an interest in meeting. The advantage here is that by having a joint association through a mutual friend, you could learn a great deal about the new person. If you find out they like football, keep that in mind should you come across tickets to a local game. Just be careful of situations where you might find yourself in a bind, leading you to decide between whom to take. Choose your opportunities wisely, and keep a list of who you may want to ask should your first pick refuse.

Not all opportunities happen easily, or as planned, but a good networker can turn any meeting with someone into a potential connection. Even while standing in line at the grocery store, being able to warmly start up a conversation with the person beside you takes skills and practice. Consider this: the person standing beside you might live in your neighborhood, they might work in an industry similar to yours, and if you make sure the people you are networking with know that you're someone that they could come to rely on, then the hard part is over. Know that in order to make good business connections you have to be good at so-called small talk. Small talk leads to bigger talks, and these big talks can lead to big opportunities.

Until you've become confident enough to socialize with just about anyone, starting conversations with complete strangers just about *anywhere*, there are places where a person can get to know someone, which can serve as practice and as a real networking opportunity. One instance is while on a plane, traveling for either business or pleasure. Think about the number of times you have to sit for hours on end beside someone. Presenting yourself as a warm, interesting person who is genuinely interested in knowing about the person sitting beside you certainly creates potential for developing a relationship with them. As always, read the person, and figure out if they seem to want to swap information, but always remain respectful. If you're uncertain, ask if they're on LinkedIn, a website specializing in networking for professionals, and if the person offers to exchange emails, make sure to follow up later and ask how they are doing. These are just a few examples of places where you would ordinarily not seek out meeting new people but could turn into networking opportunities. Any place where you could interact with others could be places to use to find and make new connections. Some other great examples are:

- Churches;
- Small parties;
- Clubs;
- When traveling;
- Sporting events;
- Dinners;
- Concerts;
- Schools;
- Volunteering.

There are many more places where you could turn a simple meeting into a networking opportunity, but the point is to look for places where you wouldn't normally expect to make networking connections. Don't overlook places where you might only drop in for a short while, or spend extended amounts of time with others. Start small, and practice, and soon, you'll develop a whole networking mindset.

Do Something Remarkable

A large part of what makes a person successful at networking is that it requires the ability to meet new people, but also to try and be remembered by them later. This can be accomplished in many ways. Your goal should not be to go into great lengths about yourself and your accomplishments—remember, people want to know what you can do for them, and will probably not remember what you've done for yourself. By all means, tell others who you are, but keep it simple and focus on creating enough interest that they want to further pursue having a professional relationship with you.

The word "remarkable" comes from the root word "re-mark", which means to say again. If you do something remarkable, you do something that people will want to tell others about. By listening and paying attention to others, you can find out about their interests and if there's a way you can associate yourself with them, they will remember you better and want to take an interest in you. If a person says they play golf, and you have a membership to your local golf course, bringing this up will definitely interest them. You may not always have ways of impressing others, but sometimes it's more of a matter of creativity, rather than having exclusive memberships and access to special events.

For business networking, this could mean doing something within your company that no one else offers or having a unique product that they'll remember later. Being unique is what sometimes can be associated with having a 'brand' for yourself or your product, and what this basically means is that you do something in a way people remember you for.

Coming up with ways of sparking others' interest may be a challenge for some, and if doing so fails you, then focus on your professionalism. The goal here is to come across as being an expert in whatever it is you do. While this does take time—an expert is someone knowledgeable within their field—having inside information and answers to tough questions will help you appear like a true expert. You may only have been doing something for a short while, but give yourself credit for what you do know within your profession; and if you're not sure of how to do something, learn. Make it your priority to learn about your industry, your position within your company, and your company itself—these are all necessary steps in becoming an expert. Remember from chapter one that one of the best things you can offer others is information. This is a valuable resource in networking with others, and being an expert makes you a credible source for others. At the end of your initial conversation with someone, you want them to remember you for who you are and for what you can do for them.

Someone Others Can Rely On

To the untrained person, networking can sound like something that requires no effort other than being able to say hello to others. Woody Allen, the famous actor and director, is quoted as saying, "Eighty percent of success is showing up." Perhaps this is the case, but for networking, showing up is the easy part—it's knowing the next step where most people fail. Now you know, great networking requires talking to others, knowing how to turn everyday occurrences into successful networking opportunities, and doing things in a way where people will remember you.

You also know that a great deal of trust goes into making good connections, which is why you should become someone others can come to rely on. Making the connection will help introduce someone into your network, but if you're not using them when you need them, then you're not networking successfully. Having a good network does not equate to simply having a large list of contacts to call on when the need arises—another misconception of networking—and too many times, a person will wait until they need something badly before reaching out to others.

The reason why it's important to call on your network contacts periodically is to ensure that the relationship is strong and so that others know that you're there for them to rely on. Practice giving first, by offering your help, recommendations, and advice. Sometimes a person may only need some support, and you could suggest a referral, or offer to provide solutions. Take the opportunity to give, so that you may receive when you need help from others. A network lives and breathes only when being used correctly, and when it benefits both parties.

Follow up with your contacts, call or email them, and as you've learned so far, set up dates to meet in person. Finding time within a busy schedule to meet someone may seem like an impossible task, but remember, you can use your creativity to meet with people while going out to do something fun, or while doing something you planned on doing beforehand, like going to dinner or a movie. It might mean having just a few minutes with them, to touch base on small business matters, but overall, you will seal the bond, and let them know that you're available when they need help, and that you're someone they can count on. Likewise, there might be a situation you're facing, and advice from your professional friend can help you with a problem. An active member of your network should be able to respond quickly to your phone calls and emails, and offer help when needed, and the same is expected of you.

Being Prepared

Networking Goals

Without having a clear view of what you plan to achieve when networking, you'll likely not see the benefits and full potential it has to offer. Measuring success is not as easy as simply plugging numbers into a formula, the way you would determine your return on investment (ROI). Rather, it's about understanding the value you get for the time and energy you invest in meeting new people. In other words, in networking, it's not just about whom you know, but also, about who knows you.

One of your goals when deciding to reach out to people, or deciding who to include in your network, is to evaluate whether or not a person would be worthwhile in your network. This isn't to say that only those with prestigious roles are worth considering. In fact, it would be foolish to assume that a person would not make a good networking contact based solely on their job, or appearance, or something equally trivial.

The question instead is: do they see something great in you? At the end of your conversation with someone, did they feel they could trust you, depend on you for help or advice, and remember you over the other people they met? If so, chances are, they will refer you and mention you to others.

Having the right goals in place will make networking more successful, and thus, more enjoyable for you. Moreover, a successful networking campaign is about knowing where to best invest networking time, and knowing how to connect with people. Joining clubs, going to lunch with friends, or attending reunions can all be places a person might meet potential network contacts so long as going to these activities helps you in return, thus fulfilling the true definition of a functioning network.

Choosing Events

A key factor in setting networking goals is to use your time wisely when choosing which networking events to attend. Planning ahead pays big dividends in the networking world, and knowing who will be in attendance makes all the difference. Out of all the people you'll likely meet, make it your objective to engage with those whom you would like to know, or may offer value to your networking circle. As you meet new people, the more information you have beforehand, the better you'll be able to understand them and relate to them, and the better your chances will be of developing a relationship with them.

After narrowing down which specific events to attend, know that there are different characteristics within the networking groups, conferences, meetings, and online networking events that you'll likely engage in. Something important to consider would be that small, formal events, such as dinners, or large gatherings, such as sports events and corporate functions, will require a different set of goals. A smaller event would allow you to know more about the people you are interacting with, whereas with a larger event trying to learn something about the hundreds of attendees could prove to be impossible. With larger events, planning can still help you target specific persons or types of people that you would like to meet. Overall, time spent networking takes away from time that could be used for other productive aspects of doing business. Thus, choose events where you're familiar with the industry, as you will know what type of people to expect, and because sharing knowledge is a key to good networking, your insight will help you make the right connections. Have some knowledge of the event itself, and if possible, familiarize yourself with the agenda so that you may plan your schedule in a way that lets you meet with others. Determining whether or not attending a function will provide you with new contacts may or may not go as planned, but make the most out of any networking event you attend by striking up conversations with people while waiting in line, or sitting beside someone. Choosing the right events is paramount, and making good connections is an effect of attending the right events.

The Elevator Hook

There are several terms for the 30-second introduction, or elevator pitch. Some people simply call it a hook—your shot to introduce who you are in just a sentence or two, with an attempt at making an impression on the person you meet. Considering that networking is something that takes time, building relationships and keeping in touch with those within your network, the likelihood of meeting someone in an elevator and making a network connection are pretty slim. Where the elevator hook does come in handy, however, is to give you the opportunity to introduce who you are in a simple, short, and effective way.

A good introduction begins with a friendly handshake. Telling someone who you are and what you do is important; you just don't want to go into any long details, or talk about yourself at great lengths—not right away. Instead, practice describing who you are in one jargon-free line about what you do. When doing so, be specific, clear, and say it in a way where the person will remember you—be remarkable.

Example:

Instead of saying:

I'm a car salesman.

Say:

I'm a salesman of all-terrain vehicles, servicing the northeast.

The second example tells 'what' you sell, 'where' you sell and effectively tells the person what you do in a way that makes you stand out from other 'ordinary' car salesmen.

Here's another example:

Instead of saying:

I work in a factory.

Say:

I assemble parts for the largest air compressor manufacturer in the country.

Again, there's no need to lie, or fabricate the truth to try and sound important, but learn about your company or industry, and point out significant aspects about what you do that make you appear experienced, knowledgeable, or notably better than others in your field.

One more example:

Instead of saying:

I'm a writer.

Say:

I'm an author of several books specializing in science fiction and military suspense.

The second option tells a lot more about the writer than the first example and can help the person you're meeting understand exactly who you are and what you have to offer them. In this case, the person you're meeting might be considering working with a writer of a different genre, or they might know someone to whom they can refer you. These are just a few examples, but if you keep your introduction short, and specific, you're more likely to be remembered later.

By using your good listening skills, find ways to segue into common-ground areas of the conversation on areas of either personal or business-related interests. As you develop your networking skills, your conversation skills will improve, and with practice, you'll develop confidence over time. Treat each new person you meet with respect, and refrain from prejudging others. Effective networking requires patience and an open mind.

Be Prepared With Questions

It's important to balance your conversation between speaking and listening while letting others talk. Something that happens far too often is that after introductions, both parties are left standing there, not knowing what to say next. After you've introduced yourself, be prepared by having a few planned, open-ended questions ready to ask.

Some examples might be:

Is this your first time to this event?

What brings you here?

How did you find out about this event?

How did you get into what you're doing?

Are you attending the event next month?

The aforementioned questions will get the person to talk about themselves, and at least one thing the two of you have in common—that you're both attending the same event. The final example offers a potential to meet again at another event, and shows the person that you're committed to networking and attend networking events regularly. Someone who attends events regularly is likely to be a good point of contact. If the person you're meeting enjoys networking, you're on the right path in having something in common with your new business friend.

Avoid common, conventional questions that people tend to ask out of politeness, without any regard to the subject itself, like, 'How are you doing?', 'How's it going?' or even asking questions like, 'You like coming here?' which may make you appear to be un-interested in the event. You want to avoid appearing negative, so refrain from commenting on the long line at the restroom or other such comments. Follow general office rules, and avoid subjects involving religion, politics, and sexual orientation, or anything else controversial for that matter. Make it your goal to have a great plan for introducing yourself, having open-ended questions that allow the person to talk about the nature and inspirations behind their business. Also, understanding someone's career path will help provide valuable insight about the person you're meeting. Starting a dialogue with others not only helps initiate a good relationship, provides valuable information about them, and helps to show your interest in someone, but also is far more effective than simply stating your verbal résumé.

Protocols and Etiquette

Expanding your set of business friends requires good communications skills and a genuine attempt to want to help others. Keep in mind that you don't want to focus too much about yourself, and also don't concentrate on titles and credentials right away. The person you meet for the first time doesn't care so much *who* you are, but rather, is interested in what you can do for them. In order to make a good impression on someone you're meeting for the first time, it's important to earn their trust. Don't make things up, or create a fake persona—the truth will arise eventually, as we can find out more information about one another easily thanks to the internet—and people can sense when someone is being genuine or not.

Unlike many of the other things a person would do throughout the day, working while eating lunch, sending emails while interacting on Facebook, talking on the phone while cooking dinner, when speaking to someone face to face, it's important to treat the person you're meeting with respect, and keep your attention focused on them. Looking over your shoulder, or checking your watch or phone makes you appear to be uninterested in the person standing in front of you, and showing someone you can successfully dedicate a few uninterrupted minutes of your time to something important will show you're dedicated and responsible, and make the person feel good about speaking with you.

As with any networking opportunity, remember to remain professional and put your best foot forward. Meeting new people, making a good impression, and asking to connect with new people you meet with hopes of walking away with their contact information means nothing if you don't follow up with them soon afterwards. If a person doesn't offer their contact information, do not stalk them on social media and insist on chatting—this is rude and aside from coming off as desperate, it could potentially drive the person away completely. If you do receive their business card, or are asked to look them up later, call or email them a week later to make sure the contact info you have is correct. Once you've established the relationship, ensure you don't neglect to maintain the relationship with your contact. Remember as much as you can about your contact and be specific when contacting them, and when choosing to meet them again, another valuable step of the networking process.

Where to Start

Friends and Family

Now that you understand networking better, how should you proceed further? Friends and family are good starting points for expanding your network because they already know you—they know what you do and can probably testify to the quality of your work and your trustworthiness. Teachers, salespersons, customer service reps, and managers, are just some of the good examples of family members who may be able to help you network more effectively.

Don't be afraid to think outside the immediate circle of friends and family, and rekindle old relationships. After college, you may have noticed that an old classmate of yours is now an intern at a large corporation, or managing a large scale project for a company, or might even be a small business owner. Possibilities exist in any of these situations. The great thing about connecting with past friends is that sharing information with them can also be fun. How about meeting them for a cup of coffee on a Saturday morning, or going for drinks after work on a Friday night, all while creating a great networking circle.

The same possibilities apply to you too when reaching out to your networking friends; is there an event for professionals that you are attending, which can benefit others? Send an email to an old friend to tell that you'll be attending this particular event, and explain how they would benefit from joining in too. It can be a good idea to ask them, but you must be careful with friends and family to never pressure them, as these people already care about you and are willing to do anything to help you out. By extending your invitations to events, it shows that you're a professional, willing to work on improving your professional relationships and also want to provide your friends a chance to expand their own networking circles as well.

Even with last minute invites, chances are that for someone to stop what they're doing and have the opportunity to go socialize with other professionals can be a fun, spur-of-moment experience, and knowing that they will likely meet other amazing people such as themselves can be exhilarating. In the end, making an effort to connect with others will have a lasting impression on your friends and family, and as the adventurous-types tend to say, when you look back from now, which would you regret not doing: taking the trip, or staying home to watch television?

Through your friends and family you have great opportunities of meeting other exciting people, and gain the experience and practice needed to improve your networking skills, all while performing the actual deed of networking itself.

Imagine meeting a friend of your cousin's, a girl named Sandy who is a yoga instructor at a gym you've never visited. Sandy is someone within your area, and she later opens her own class in a small shopping strip near your house. You run into Sandy at the grocery store and at that point realize you hadn't exchanged information with her, but because she's so excited about having her own place to teach yoga right near your house, you offer to go there, and she gives you her phone number. After calling her later that very day, you invite her to cocktails one evening at your house and, while there, she meets several people that are looking for a yoga class to attend. Sandy also meets John, a painter who will paint her studio at a great price.

See how quickly networking works at bringing people to-gether in a way that can work toward mutual benefits and open opportunities for both parties involved?

Your Own Organizations

If waiting for an event to occur does not work and it appears that the opportunities are simply not there, then make your own oppor-tunities by creating events for others to attend. Sometimes this can be as simple as having drinks or inviting others to meet you for din-ner, or the theater, or other hobbies that may interest you. Do you play sports? Great. Sporting activities are fun avenues for meeting others. Engaging in activities that others enjoy doing as well, you will establish relationships with people that share the same inter-ests you do.

Starting networking organizations can require some addi-tional income if done as a non-profit, or as a business within itself or a registered club. If you're already a small business owner, the organization can simply be held within your business or within someone else's business to include classes, workshops, and demonstrations. Sometimes networking organizations can include forming a group for the purpose of tackling problems within an in-dustry, or to create a startup or develop small business ideas. A networking organization can also be informal, fun gatherings. For example, a person who likes camping can form a group of people who go hiking and camping once a year in a way that is both enjoy-able and works to tie relationships together with others within their network. With starting an organization, you may require the services of different people, and by doing so, it allows the people within your organization to help others, and make their services available, and open opportunities for everyone within the organi-zation. The key to building your own networking organization or hosting events is to allow others to build everlasting relationships.

Your Field of Business

There are lots of ways to connect with people, and one of the most effective ways is to speak to others within the same industry as you. By meeting with other like-minded people, sharing ideas and offering each other support and help, lots of network growth can happen, as the parties involved trade business ideas and teach each other new skills. One important thing to consider is the potential for new career opportunities when the time arises. Needing to fill a position in a hurry is a frequent occurrence, and finding qualified candidates costs time and money, as managers or HR specialists post ads, search through potential resumes, and interview potential candidates. Hiring someone can cost more money when hiring through a temp agency, which do a lot of the work for the hiring company as part of their service.

A networking friend could easily say, 'I know Joe and he fits all the qualifications and would make a great addition to the company.' The chances of a referral being hired are upward of 80% according to surveys conducted by ABC News, and there's a good reason for it. A person who is already employed somewhere is probably a good worker, and being they have good work ethics, they will likely recommend someone who would make a good employee. It is expected that a good employee would recommend someone with the intent of maintaining their own good reputation.

Keeping contacts within your industry may keep you in the loop with industry news. Friends in similar industries can also be someone to call on when in a bind—for instance, if a customer of yours needs a particular product the vendor might be out of, and a simple call might get you out of a jam. There are many possibilities, and they're made possible by keeping good networking relationships with others.

Reaching out to others may require turning old enemies into friends, or offering to help others with no intentions of receiving a reward. Learn to depend on those in your industry with knowledge about the products you sell or services you offer. Ask questions, as the smartest people tend to know how important it is to have others to rely on when you need help. Businesses today are not structured the way they were just a few decades ago, because companies today can be so large and complicated, that it becomes difficult for someone to have all the information they need to do their job efficiently. In the business world, sharing is a good practice that helps everyone make better decisions. Asking for help is a great way to establish relationships as well as make you more efficient at your job. You'd be surprised: more people are receptive and willing to help than you would imagine, and often, the kindness of others is given no credit. For some, it's not easy to ask others for help, as they may fear that it makes them appear unknowledgeable. Others may fear that by asking for help, they appear to be lazy or unmotivated, but that couldn't be farther from the truth. Seeking information from others not only provides clarification, such as explanations and procedures, but also will help prevent inefficiency, as no one can afford to do the same job twice. Networking is not often seen as a way of meeting new people but it also means sharing information and maintaining proactive relationships with others within their network.

Just as keeping good networking relationships within your industry can carry with it many great advantages, another great source for branching out your network is to look at sectors similar to yours or even sectors that have no direct relation, but that may have individuals with knowledge and expertise that you may be interested in.

In the past, having a good network was viewed as a privilege of the affluent, and not spoken of or taken seriously by most professionals. Today, networking is a must-have, and the relationships you build will create life-long benefits and opportunities. Just keep in mind that building a strong network requires interactions on your part that may require you to set up events, make referrals, introduce new people to your colleagues, and assist your circle in any way you can.

Making the Right Connections

Key People

Some people have natural networking gifts, and this is evident by their charisma and radiant smiles. They tend to know just about everyone and spark interest in others at every party or social event, capturing the attention and minds of all the thinkers in the room. They know everyone's name and can make introductions quickly. They are considered to have the right attitude and are charming and engaging. These characteristics mark the type of personality that would identify a 'key' person within your network. This is someone who knows how to bring people together, and they serve as a vital component to improve your ability to connect with others in unfamiliar circles.

What can be learnt from key people in networking is that they have the ability to talk to anyone, including people they've never met before, and most of them have a knack for talking—something others tend to require an effort to do. It's a unique gift, and while practice will improve anyone's ability to introduce themselves and have flowing conversations with total strangers, some are just born with this talent for being the working wheels of the ethos engine.

An easy way to spot a key person is to stop and think of the individuals you know who would easily approach you and offer advice, or would make recommendations about your work, or may have even made referrals about you to someone else. Not all great networking friends have to fit the description of key people; in fact, remember the colleague at work selling Girl Scout cookies? That person may just be a coworker from whom you buy cookies or slices of cake and sweetbread once a year; but keep in mind that networking opportunities happen through all channels, and there are chances for relationships to begin and grow through each channel.

Suppose your coworker has a husband who's an artistic painter, and you know of a friend who started an art gallery-style website. Well, there you go. You make a referral, and they decide to meet and now your coworker is linked to friends of yours, and in the process of it all, your coworker will remember you and keep you in mind when the time comes that she needs help.

If you're sitting at dinner with a group of people and you want to improve your chances of making good connections, by all means, sit beside a key person and watch how many times they bring you up or include you into the conversation. At the end of the night you will likely be remembered and feel more confident in yourself than you had otherwise, allowing you to reach out and make friends with the guests at your dinner party. Don't simply rely on your key people to do all the talking; it's still up to you to participate. Meeting others and creating network contact involves showing your ability to converse in a reciprocal sharing of information and resources. A person who says too little, or is stingy with their information or unwilling to provide insight, may soon find themselves out of the loop. Try to balance your amount of listening with the number of times you speak, and be attentive, which can help you notice certain speaking points where you can contribute and help enrich the conversation.

Knowing Who is Who

It's important that within any industry, you familiarize yourself with influential individuals who play important roles at all business levels. Start with your place of work; know who the boss is and who *his* boss is, and so on. If you ever meet, it's important to be able to address them correctly, especially considering that they may not recognize you, even after having met in the past. While it may be okay for the boss to get away with not recognizing others—this depends on who you ask—nothing could be more embarrassing for someone who is trying to get themselves known, than introducing themselves again to someone they may have already met. Not only is it embarrassing, but makes you appear selfish and unreceptive, and this can then translate into appearing to be someone who doesn't care. For someone trying to enhance their career, or social circle, it can be a costly move as you lose valuable connections but also make the version of yourself the world sees appear unprofessional.

Within all your social groups, knowing who is who means knowing *who* does *what*. This is something to consider when relying on your network for advice or help. Before going to any of your business friends asking for favors, ensure that you have offered and preferably done something for them before. This is where meeting others for dinners and events comes in handy. A person feels they know you well the more they interact with you, and now it's simply a matter of doing a favor for a friend; not doing so because they're being used or because they expect something in return.

When attending networking events, knowing who is who means quickly memorizing the names and faces of the people you meet. Make yourself notes if you have to, explaining who you have met and whether you have any contact info on them. Watch for details and indicators that can assist you in knowing that particular person's likes, dislikes interests or hobbies. Choose appropriate topics when interacting; for example, for someone who is a cricketer or baseball player with a community team, talking movies or technology may not hold their interest. The same goes for those who work in specific fields. If a professional you know is in the technology sector, they may not keep up with your favorite sports team, so the key is to pick up on details that reveal areas of interest that others may like. Since networking is a mutual exchange of help, over the long-term, make it your goal to figure out what you can offer to those in your circle, and interact with your contacts in fruitful ways. Foremost, knowing just a few bits of information about a contact can give you a big advantage in establishing a strong relationship. Once you have some details , update your contact information, making notes describing who they are, or what they do, and this will help make remembering them easier, but also will make searching them in your contacts a breeze. Taking the time to know your contacts well is essential for being able to introduce them to new circles quickly and confidently, while making a good impression, starting with the very first introduction. Before follow up meetings with contacts, look through your contact information and refresh your memory—being prepared will ensure you stay on top of your networking skills. Your network revolves around a cycle of establishing, expanding, and maintaining your set of business friends, so take the time to meet with your contacts on a regular basis.

Face-to-Face Communications

Throughout the course of history, people have preferred the most personal form of interaction over any other: face-to-face communication. Today, social media sites have millions of members, and more people interact with other users on these sites than ever before; however, trends change, people change, the popularity of websites change, and face-to-face relationships will probably outlast any other method of socializing. Showing up to an event, and taking the time to meet other people, shows you're responsible, lets others know that you're attentive, and demonstrates to others that you can be intuitive to their needs.

When engaging in face-to-face conversation, a person does two things: they communicate verbally, and they communicate non-verbally. While having good verbal communication is important—there are certain ideas or opinions or sentiments that can be said more clearly with words—there is something inherently powerful about non-verbal communication. Expressing your feelings for someone who has lost a loved one, for example, would allow the person to see your sincerity, as you show sorrow using tone of voice, hand gestures and facial expressions, whereas the same words in an email would not have the same significance. A large part of what happens when meeting someone face-to-face happens on a subconscious level, and there are several reasons why it affects you differently than other forms of communication.

Physical conversations with potential contacts allows a deeper level of connection with someone new than months of social media interaction and no face-to-face communication ever could. Generally, a person wants to see facial expressions, study mannerisms and have that *feeling good* sensation about the person they're speaking to. Quite simply, the feelings and emotions another person can detect in your face can tell others if you're happy, sad, surprised, angry, shy, guilty, or can show others other attributes like shame, fear, contempt, and let others know when you're truly interested, or irritated. Furthermore, your body also expresses emotions or can tell others about your personality. Your movements or posture can show you to be physically energetic, experiencing nervousness if you're fidgeting or clenching your hands, or can express your warmness with the use of friendly touches.

Other characteristics of your personality include: choice of words, the rate at which you speak, and the volume of your voice. People with louder, deeper voices can be seen as competent and honest, or as uncompromising and aggressive, in some cases. On the other hand, people with immature voices may be seen as less experienced, or less powerful, while a person with a soft voice can be seen as honest and warm. Believe it or not, your voice can be measured by others and your attractiveness can be based on tempo, rhythm, and clarity. Those with attractive voices tend to appear as having the ability to draw people in, pleasing others, and being able to win.

Moreso, a person watches another when speaking with an aim at making an emotional connection. This goes back to what was discussed in Chapter 1, that a person wants to be able to trust you before wanting to do business with you. Therefore, your ability to show others, both verbally and physically, that you're being sincere with your intentions will help create the types of relationships that are imperative to creating a sound, functioning network. Whether or not your speaking level is where you want it to be, stick to being able to produce quality speech in your verbal and non-verbal communications. This includes using euphemisms and kinder words in place of offensive or rude language. You should also avoid using words that allow the other person to insinuate there's a hidden purpose to what you're saying, and instead be clear and honest in your speech. For the sake of speaking more powerfully, avoid using hesitations or fillers such as: "uh", "I guess", "kind of", "you know and 'like', which can make you appear inexperienced or even immature.

Overall, learn to identify key people to have in your network. Having one or two can make a big difference in the amount of exposure you have with new and prospective contacts. If you're working to build your network from the ground up, start with friends and family and use your time networking with them to practice improving your networking skills. Go out and talk to neighbors or individuals in your community, but know who is who and learn to remember important details about your contacts. Understand the importance of face-to-face communication and while social media is an integral part of today's social behavior, use social media to reinforce your relationships, but not to replace valuable networking practices like meeting in person. If you still think Facebook is as effective as face-to-face networking, ask yourself, how many of your online contacts do you engage with regularly? Probably very few, and of those few, how many have you been able to rely on for help? An emoji might depict your current state of happiness, but it can't replace the feeling someone gets when being greeting instead by a firm handshake.

Managing Your Network

Build Exceptional Resources

Rising through the ranks typically requires a person to have a strong understanding of the business at hand, to work hard and, probably most importantly, to know where to go when needing support, feedback, and information. Overall, it's any leader's job to tackle tough problems, and, while doing so, he or she does require a respectable level of smarts and understanding. There's also a non-tactical aspect of problem solving that comes from knowing how to use your resources. Within each group of contacts, there are skilled and talented individuals who will assist you with prioritizing tasks and will offer support and suggestions regarding the challenges you face. Having access to such valuable assets lives at the heart of all leadership roles, and, not surprisingly, for every manager who has successfully constructed a strong network, there are dozens who fail to overcome their obstacles.

Effective leaders learn to employ their networking resources for constructive purposes. Similar to the key people mentioned in Chapter 7, if you have exceptional members within your network, this would bring added knowledge and a wealth of experience, which act as valuable resources to help you accomplish your goals. Just as it's important to understand which networking events will benefit you most, you also should know how to selectively choose people within your network who will provide you with assistance when you need it.

While the idea may seem insincere or even selfish, you must grasp the idea that a person with functional specialties will be a high stakeholder within your network. It *does* pay to know people in high places. Your friends in high places are there because of their success. Although you shouldn't look to them for financial support, you can learn about their good business habits and discover strategies for success. As the media mogul Oprah once said, "Surround yourself with only people who are going to lift you higher." That very concept is the basis for many motivational business speeches and books, and it happens to be a distinct and vital role in networking.

At the same time, don't network with only the most successful people you know. Having a strong network requires having people in it from different walks of life, with varied talents and respective sets of friends. Your exceptional business friends will have great advice to offer, but remember that they are also hard-working people. You should be willing to support them as well, just as you should with everyone in your network. When determining whom you value most within your network, ask yourself what you could be doing to help your colleagues, and then ask yourself, is there anything they can do to help me? The key is to help your network first, and your reward will come later.

Your networking relationships will vary from person to person, but by knowing who your most helpful business friends are, you can exercise discretion over who gets more of your attention, to ensure that your friendship ties are strong and to help you maintain high-quality relationships. With large networks, the constraints of knowing where to harness your energy means focusing on relationships that are likely to deliver more value. Your most valuable contacts are your exceptional resources, and they will provide you with more assistance, information, and guidance than other people you may have connected with. If all of your networking contacts are so helpful as to be considered exceptional, then you'll have no trouble finding the help you need when you need it.

Meet Your Influencers

Passing up great opportunities happens all too often, and the reason for not going is usually a reluctance to step out of one's comfort zone. While it's not necessary to attend every event you're invited to, as you now know, choosing your events wisely will pay off. Sometimes, even when the event does not quite fit your schedule, if it's publicized that a highly influential person will attend, you should make an effort to attend. A highly influential person can be someone famous, such as an actor or singer, or even a politician with power, but it's not limited to the famous. It can be a well-known person in your industry or a successful person you've heard about, or it can be someone that you'd simply like to meet because you've heard great things about them and they inspire—hence influence—you to do better and succeed. It's a good time to remember Oprah's saying about surrounding yourself with successful people—which is the basis for books like *Rich Dad, Poor Dad*—but few people realize that in order to do so, one must first have good networking skills. Not only should you include people who are successful in your network, but you should also include people who will encourage and inspire you.

Staying Organized

Once upon a time, back when the original G.I. Joe was still a popular Saturday morning cartoon and kids everywhere grasped the concept that 'Knowing is half the battle,' business people sat at their metallic desks, staring at tiny, DOS-based screens and flipped through a Rolodex when needing to locate a contact. In concept, it was and still is a great idea: having all your contacts in one easy to find, organized location. Today, keeping track of your contacts and network data can be discouraging, especially when it's spread over multiple systems such as personal email, business email, Facebook, LinkedIn, Twitter, and about a half dozen other sources. Getting yourself organized will take some of the effort and hard work out of networking, and with the right help, anyone can take control of their contact database.

Today, most email providers now offer great tools for organizing emails, calendars, and contacts. Probably one of the easiest to use is Gmail, with its ability to sync contacts from places such as Facebook and other social media sites. Google also offers a great feature called "multiple inboxes" in which a person can create several inboxes and sort them by contact, or content, and can recognize and separate important messages from the bulk of your email. The marked emails will show up in one of the inboxes above your normal inbox to ensure you see it immediately, making it easy to keep track of messages from anyone. There are other features within Gmail that automatically sort your messages with labels, sending emails directly to specific folders, keeping them out of your inbox, but making them available to view as you please. Two other great apps that you might find useful and will make organizing fun are Todoist (https://en.todoist.com) and Evernote, (https://evernote.com).

Todoist is a To-do list app that makes adding notes to your calendar a cinch. Back in the Rolodex days, people carried little notebooks around and wrote down all the activities they needed to accomplish that day. This practice—writing down short-term goals—has been exalted and followed by successful people for ages, but now, with Todoist, adding an event or reminder is easy and the cool part is that the event stays in your Todoist inbox until you check it off, keeping you actively marking off your goals. To use it, you simply type in the event and time in one simple line and when Todoist is synced to your Google calendar, you will be sent a reminder at the time of the event, should you decide to turn on your phone notifications on your mobile app. Think of how easy it could be to keep track of networking events, meetings, and making yourself reminders to return calls or emails. Todoist also allows you to easily postpone or change items in your box for another day, week or month, but having to check them off is really the motivating tool that makes working with the app fun and keeps you motivated to finish your tasks for the day.

Evernote is another great app with a clean-looking platform and easy to use features that makes it a combination of note keeping, project management and a place to set up reminders. The app serves as a blank canvas you can easily access either online or through a mobile app, where you assign project names to your notebooks and make notes that can include charts, web links, and other interesting gadgets to help keep all your ideas in a tidy, easy-to-access place. Use Evernote to make notes on your contacts and networking events, or practically anything you'd like. It's great for someone on the go and perfect for plans or ideas that are too long to put in a calendar, or for someone who just wants to make notes to themselves, jot down ideas for a project, or keep track of other important reminders. Since Evernote can also sync to google calendar, project or event reminders made within Evernote will show up as reminders on your mobile device, making planning and managing your own events a piece of cake.

While there are several great forms of email available today to help you organize contacts, a great option to consider is Microsoft Outlook. Outlook can be downloaded for free and sync to other email accounts such as Gmail and Yahoo and is great at syncing contacts from across several email addresses and social media sites. Not all social media sites and email hosts will be available to sync with Outlook, but some of the most popular are. With the purchase of Office 365, you also get access to OneDrive, a cloud based platform for storing files with a few more professional features than Evernote, where you can use OneNote to organize ideas.

If email organization is your thing, there's another app called Cloze (https://www.cloze.com) that helps you organize contacts, but one of its coolest features is the way it helps organize your email account and social media feeds. For someone who has tons of Facebook friends and Twitter followers, Cloze can be a saving grace in that it recognizes, based on your history, who the important contacts are in your network, which will send a Facebook post, tweet, or email to the top of your inbox to ensure you don't miss anything from the people you need to connect with. Cloze has both a free version and a finely-tuned optimized one with a few more features, including filters to help you keep tabs on all your networking friends.

Even in this day and age—one relatively free of the Rolodex—there's still the question of what to do with business cards when someone hands you one. While the information on business cards is valuable, finding a business card when you need it becomes a hassle of searching through cluttered desk drawers and file cabinets, but with the Scannable app (https://evernote.com/products/scannable/), a product of Evernote, you can scan business cards with your mobile device's camera and keep their information handy on the Evernote app.

Simply snap a photo and file it away, which will make keeping track of your stack of business cards at your next conference or trade show much easier. If you have to skip all the technically savvy methods of importing business cards into an app, at least take the few minutes it takes to create a contact into your phone using a business card—that way you will have it handy when you need it. See that you're entered as a contact as well—you never know, the next time someone might need you, a great opportunity may pass by because your business card got buried in a file drawer some-where. Just remember, how well you manage your professional network is critical to becoming a master networker. Making use of the tools available can make this process so much easier.

Branding and Online Presence

Establishing a Brand

Everyone has a brand, but not everyone is aware of it. Everything you do and say makes an impression on those around you, and not taking the time to create the right brand could turn out to be a big mistake in the long run.

But what is a brand?

Simply put, a "brand" is a mixture of the characteristics that others will remember you by. What you display about yourself creates your brand, and for those who think they can choose not to have one, a brand is created for you either intentionally or unintentionally.

Establishing a brand for yourself is not a gimmick, nor is it a long, drawn out process with something to prove, but it does require making an earnest attempt at trying to be genuine. What this means is, you may have skills, or abilities, or something within your personality that you can turn into an opportunity that can help you stand out.

If you're an expert in your field, that would be considered part of your brand. Do you know history, science, math, and can make references, solve problems in your head, or do you love sports or shows where singers compete for a shot at becoming famous? Believe it or not, all those things are part of your brand. Your brand should be made up of all the parts that make you tick. Your interests, hobbies, your career, and even the people within your network all help create a unique person that others can remember. For instance, if you're someone who knows a lot about animals, people will ask you questions about their pets, and being an animal-person will become part of your brand. Are you great with watches, and everyone in the office asks you to change their watch batteries, or they want your opinion on a particular model before making a purchase? Then being a watch person is part of your brand. Same goes for cars, carpentry, cleaning pools, flying model planes, or operating camera-mounted drones—you name it, if it's a hobby or interest or basically anything you're good at, then it will become part of what establishes you as you.

Your brand is most likely also part of your heritage. If you're from a particular country, you might be expected to know how to make a native dish, or tell others about the culture and history of your country.

A great way to establish your brand with potential contacts is by creating a version of yourself that stands out and makes a positive impression. If you have multiple talents, concentrate on a few and utilize them in unique ways to assist your network. Ensuring others know where your best talents lie will help them remember you. Good networking involves helping others, and when people know what it is you have to offer them, you'll be someone they can easily remember to come to for help or advice.

While you may not be able to control what society thinks of you, know that you definitely have a choice to act in a way where people know what to expect of you. Just as having positive characteristics can make a good impression, having negative characteristics will have an adverse effect.

Not coming through when expected, or having a negative outlook, may let others know that you're not someone they want to rely on in the future. Your brand is essentially your promise to your contacts, and every person you meet, every phone call you make, every email you send, will represent you, your brand, and your promise. Your brand will establish you as being someone forgettable—or someone remarkable.

Making Yourself Easy to Find

During the late 1990s, the dot-com boom was in full swing and the bubble that would soon after pop was merely in its early stages of growth. It was thought back then that all businesses would turn to e-commerce, and that *anyone* who wanted to make it in the future would need a strong online presence. Technology was improving, the internet was becoming easily accessible to everyone, and websites were growing at a rapid rate. In the end, investors poured money into too many internet startups, and the market collapsed. But what came from the boom of e-companies was that, eventually, the internet would enable billions of people around the world to have easy access to information on any subject or just about any product imaginable.

Fifteen years ago only the most cutting-edge companies had websites. But today, now that you can obtain a website for free, anyone can form an easy way for others to learn about you and what you do. Today, the first thing people do when they want to learn about a product, service, or a topic is to use a search engine like Google. Having a website not only gives you a sense of legitimacy—that is, it establishes who you are—but it also allows online users to know that you have a means by which to communicate with them and that you're someone they can rely on for help. Having an online presence is more important than ever as the general public has come to rely on the internet for so many things over the past decade. With so many free options available, it's easier than ever to start your own website, and with sites like *http://www.weebly.com*, *http://www.wix.com*, and *https://wordpress.com*, you can start easily and quickly.

Choosing a website that's easy to find is essential. Sometimes it takes a little creativity when your full name is already taken. Try choosing a combination of your name and what you do: *Frankthepumber.com* or something with just a little more creativity will work. The key is to make yourself recognizable to anyone trying to find you, should it be a potential networking contact, a client, or anyone else.

If you're on multiple social media websites, uniformity can help others verify who you are. This could be accomplished by posting the same headshot across all your sites, for example. Finding ways to make yourself unmistakably recognizable will make it easier for others to connect with you, and you can even assign a look to go with your brand. Similar to the way product brands are associated with logos, designs, and colors, you too can make your website revolve around a certain icon or color scheme, or again, by simply using the same photo of yourself.

Most people don't like promoting themselves, but with a good website, and with a good brand, you can allow the internet to do the promotional work for you. Your website is a great place to write about your passions or experiences, and you'd be surprised by the number of online users who would be interested in what you have to say. If you've figured out the solution to a problem, you could blog about it as a way to help other bloggers. Just keep in mind that if you do blog, you will likely need to keep your content fresh, and blog regularly, or risk losing readers or fail to attract new readers. Don't use blogging to pitch products but instead to meet new contacts and grow your network. Respond to questions and comments, and show your willingness to help readers and other bloggers whenever possible. Generosity goes a long way when networking, and online users will remember you for 'being there' for them when they needed it. Giving advice and sharing your time can be some of the greatest resources you have to offer.

For professionals, websites are the new business cards, but even for someone fresh out of college who is looking to find their way into a new career, having a website establishing who you are, what kind of activities you do, or which organizations you belong to, and explaining that you're looking for a job, can help potential employers connect with you. By including your web page on your resume, employers can find out more about you by quickly searching for you online.

But let's make a clear distinction between the two: establishing a good brand will help people remember you, while having an online presence simply makes your information easier to access.

Content That Generates Buzz

Creating a brand means letting others know where your expertise lies. This can include your hobbies, or other topics your website or blog revolves around. You want to make sure that the content you choose is new, fresh, and interesting. Therefore, if all you have to say about making cookies is the same as what's already online, no one would remember having read or learned anything from your site. Instead, trying new ingredients, or a different way of shaping or baking the cookies that make them more fun to eat, or taste better than the ones people already make, will help generate buzz about your topic.

The focal point of Seth Godin's book, *Purple Cow*, is that a product or company must be unique to make it in today's market. Godin gives examples about how being outlandish and even offensive is better than being bland and mundane because, by being unique, you generate buzz about your product or service, and this works as a marketing device to help your company expand. However, these tactics may not apply to networking, as you're trying to earn the respect of contacts so that they listen and trust you and, in the end, want to develop a meaningful relationship with you. When networking, being controversial may not always have a positive effect on the way you promote yourself, but the point behind *Purple Cow* is this: people remember unique.

Search Engine Optimization (SEO) Content

Doing business online these days demands some knowledge of SEO. When you sign up to create a website, you'll see options for improved searches that require using key words meant to direct online users to your website. For example, if you're a biology major looking to find a career doing research at a lab, you include words that associate you with the type of work you'd like to do, such as, *lab technician,* or *scientific research*, or include the names of the diseases you've worked with, or the schools you went to.

Over 500 million people carry out searches on Google every day, and while you may think that people would not come across your site, SEO helps your site appear to people at the perfect time they're looking for it. As useful as it may sound, SEO options come at different prices, so be prepared to pay for good SEO. Depending on how you plan to use it, advanced SEO may well be worth the cost. The key to using SEO words isn't necessarily choosing words that are located on the website, but instead to think of what the user may be searching for in relation to your page. For a person who sells surfboards, the number of people searching surfboards may be low, but they could play to a larger potential crowd by choosing words with similarities, like appearing to those searching for beaches.

Of course, there is no magic snake oil that will bring people to your site fast; drawing attention to any website usually takes time. By some standards, SEO should be changed frequently, but give your SEO content a couple months to adequately measure the change in traffic, or 'hits' as they're called. In some cases, increases in traffic take as little as a couple of weeks, but usually they take time. To take a view at what people are searching for, try

BuzzSumo (http://buzzsumo.com/). In this easy to use website, you simply type in a word to see what types of searches are being conducted in relation to those specific words. The search tool on BuzzSumo can also show how many times something has been shared on Facebook or Twitter, and can help you improve your SEO options. Overall, most webhosting domains allow SEO features, but as mentioned before, they come at a price. For those who would rather rely on a professional for help, SEO agencies can offer their services to help increase the number of visitors, but most agencies, aside from being expensive, offer no guarantees. For someone looking to improve their network, paying big bucks for SEO may not be the best move, but for other purposes it's a handy feature.

Facebook

Why Use Facebook?

Facebook is the most popular social media website in the world. Its popularity has soared over the years to a total of 2billion users, or about 39 percent of all social network total members according to Facebook's 2017 second quarter earnings report. If it continues to grow as it has year over year, Facebook will likely reach 50 percent of all social media sometime within 2018. One day, as public tastes change, another social media site might take the number one title, but for now, Facebook dominates as the forum for interaction, and if you decide to only have one social networking site to be a member of, Facebook will give you the most exposure. Log onto any website and you're likely to find the Facebook logo somewhere on the homepage, that simple but unmistakable lower case "f" that anyone can recognize. The more people use it, the more popular it becomes, and for years the Facebook app has been on the top of the download charts, so recognize exactly the type of impact this social media giant could have on your ability to connect with online users.

Facebook acts similar to the way a website would, only it works to try and match you to people you may know and makes it easy for other users to find you. Having a Facebook page alone will probably not help you expand your network or create many opportunities for you. In fact, you shouldn't rely on websites like Facebook to try and make new contacts, instead, use it as a tool to help you gain recognition and as a way to help you plan and keep in touch with those within your network. Interacting with others online can help reinforce relationships, but true networking requires meeting with others face to face for the simple reason that the same level of openness and honesty cannot be achieved through messaging and chatting on social media. However, Facebook is a valuable tool that can let you follow up with those within your network, and allows you to schedule events, make announcements and stay informed. Within the past year, Facebook has focused more on sharing content, videos specifically, as it competes with websites such as YouTube for users, but when used correctly, Facebook is a networker's heaven.

Through sharing and communicating with online users, Facebook will help you find events and other networking activities that will help expand your network. By simply signing up to the Facebook pages of clubs and organizations available to help increase your networking circle, you can easily invite others, or let contacts know which ones you plan on attending, helping you and your networking friends join forces and grow their own networks and create opportunities for all. For anyone with a large number of people who want to share information or schedule events, Facebook is a time saver for communicating your message to others. With features like having the ability to classify your Facebook friends, you can easily create lists for anyone you wish to involve either in your messages, posts, or for sending invitations. Facebook is also one of the easiest websites to use for finding old friends and classmates, and these are exactly the types of people to consider when growing your network. For those seeking to reach a broader market than just people from the past, the social media giant also offers a great marketing tool called Facebook Ads.

What are Facebook Ads?

Now that you understand the significant reach Facebook has on the people around you, Facebook Ads can help you reach more potential contacts than just those within your networks. This tool may not be essential for someone simply looking to connect with others, but for those scheduling events, starting an organization or simply needing to draw attention to a specific product or service, be it a special cause or a particular business, Facebook Ads are a great way to potentially reach millions of users, but more importantly, through segmentation, you can even learn how to target specific users or groups of users.

Creating a Facebook Ads account is simple, and anyone with a Facebook account can do it. You simply find the dropdown box that says "create Ads" and you'll immediately be prompted to start a campaign. For an event planner, finding who you want to include could be simple, but for a business owner, knowing who to target could prove challenging, depending on how you plan to use your Ads account. Creating a strategy through segmentation, you can narrow down your targeted groups, allowing you to reach those users who would benefit most from your message.

One of the first notions to consider when cutting the pie and choosing sections to distribute your message to is the location of the people you are seeking to relay your information to. Location can be broken down by country, region, state, neighborhood, zip code or more general or specific fields to meet your likings.

Say you want to start an indoor soccer league in your city. You can create your ads to target people in your city and specific neighborhoods within the general vicinity of your selected sports facility, and draw in all the people you need to help create the league.

The same goes for someone hosting an event or conference. Giving you the ability to target professionals within a specified area will expand your reach to a specific kind of people. There are many possibilities, and because different regions partake in different activities, you attract only those you would truly be interested in your Ad. While segmenting by geographic region can work wonders for attracting people locally, when seeking international attention, segmenting would have to be organized differently.

Another choice would be to divide groups by demographic, including targeting people by categories such as gender, age, race, marital status, income, occupation, and so on. The more options you use when narrowing down a potential group of people, the more specific the outcome will be. But remember: with each cut of the pie, the piece becomes smaller. Using demographics as a choice can help draw in anyone with specific needs; for example, say you're hosting a makeup event and you choose to target women, you could go so far as to decide on a specific age group or income level, and break that list down even more if needed to. In any event, advertising to a specific demographic can draw in people by their occupation, educational level, or social class, and each of these can play a vital role in how it can affect your needs, be it you need to call on engineers for a conference, or you aim to target a specific group of people to join your club or organization. With each variable there are many possibilities.

A group of people can also be segmented by their interests or lifestyles, and focusing on these things in particular can help reach sports fans, car enthusiasts, wine drinkers, beer drinkers, those who love fishing—the list goes on and on. The great thing about Facebook Ads is that with a few simple tweaks, you can target just about anyone, and all it takes is being able to ask for the right person. Knowing who to target in the first place can be a bit tricky. Luckily, you have the option to try different things, and with easy-to-use tools located directly on Facebook, measuring your click-though rates is clear and simple.

Throughout these different categories, whether used alone or in combination with one another, you can reach any group of people imaginable. If you're creating a film show with movies based on a specific ethnicity or gender, you can easily adjust your ads to concentrate on your desired target. A large, outdoor family event can target people by lifestyle, location, or demographic, and if there's a more specific motive, detailing the type of people using all three will help draw in the exact group you'd desire. Connecting with others through Facebook Ads can draw in anyone, from builders in Costa Rica to businessmen in China and everyone in between, and attracting the people you need becomes as simple as choosing your audience with a few clicks.

Getting Started With Facebook Ads

If you already have a Facebook account that you use strictly as a personal account, you can create a new login for the sole purpose of running ads and to keep your professional contacts and posts separate from your personal ones. Combining your personal contacts with your networking contacts can make it difficult in most cases to filter posts from friends and family who are sharing either personal information, photos or videos, or those sharing posts or links that, while they may have been sent with good intentions—after all, *they* found it humorous—aren't appropriate for a professional account. Protecting yourself and your brand will help establish yourself as a professional looking to meet other professionals.

An Ad can be created by first selecting a category for your post and then uploading a photo or logo that will help people establish the content of your page. This is usually followed by writing a sentence to state your message, or include a link that will bring people to your page and you can get as creative as you want, including using video clips that will help broadcast your message. At first, you may want to start by reaching others with Facebook posts that can range from anything such as notices or announcements, to full TV commercial quality advertisements that tell people all the details of function or event. As people begin to like and click on your Ad, you will see it appear in their news feeds and this is when you can optimize your post. By choosing different types of ads to run, you essentially increase the potential to reach new contacts, as not all ads are created equal. For the most part though, keep your ads simple, as short ads, those within 100-250 characters, get about 60 percent more likes and are commented on and shared more than longer ones. Photos and other visual aspects such as fonts and color schemes can also help drive up engagement, so make your ad appealing and tasteful, focusing on a friendly approach that would be equivalent to the way someone would associate *you* to your brand.

With any advertising campaign that you run, set your goals and focus on the people you are targeting, keeping in mind that the effects will be determined based on the audience, and not on *your* likes and dislikes. Not focusing on the right group would be like taking shots in the dark, and your attempts to reach others would be made in vain. To best find the people you want, use segmentation as a tool to target people by location, demographic, or by their interests or lifestyle. Be as specific or as general as you'd like, but know that your ad will be seen by everyone, so targeting people more specifically, such as those in a single city or a certain age group, will help you reach those within your target audience.

Facebook is one of the many social media platforms to offer ad segmentation, but aside from being the largest and one of the easiest to use, the features on Facebook work well by themselves and can also work with other programs such as Qwaya (http://www.qwaya.com/), which can help streamline your ads and offer advanced targeting options that, when used correctly, will help you hone in on the right user.

Linkedin

Strictly For Professionals

Despite all the differences between young and old generations, the one thing that's growing rapidly in everyone's lives is the use of social media. For many reasons, be it chatting with friends for fun, or sharing photos, the average social media site revolves around entertainment, as people share video clips, website links and a great many "likes". But out of all the social media websites, one that stands out significantly is LinkedIn, a social networking site that focuses on professionals. Unlike Facebook, Twitter, Snapchat, and the rest, LinkedIn tends to not follow trends and instead creates a unique, purpose-driven environment with a specific goal. While Facebook has remained the social media giant for years, in spite of the competition, LinkedIn has continually added users and reported to have 500 million members as of the second quarter of 2017.

LinkedIn CEO Jeff Weiner, unknown to most, is a business-minded leader who makes it clear that LinkedIn serves a purpose other than sharing personal information and insists that the website is not, by definition, a "social network," but instead he refers to the distinct medium as a "professional network." While Facebook and other such sites are a great place for keeping in touch with friends, LinkedIn has built its platform around the ability to cater to professionals seeking to meet other professionals, and, specifically, for job-seeking professionals. This functionality has been the basis for its success along with the recent economic downturn, which served LinkedIn well, as LinkedIn grew its membership from 15 million in 2007, to over 40 million by 2009, just as the unemployment rate reached its highest during the 2007-2009 recession. As more and more members sign onto LinkedIn, it becomes a growing, powerful tool to help expand your professional network and help people improve their careers. At the rate LinkedIn has been growing, on average one new member signs up per second, or about 2 new members in the time it took you to read this sentence. Another reason for LinkedIn's increased success has been due to an ever-growing business model popular with internet-based companies over the past few years: the "freemium" model, or a free service that offers more features at a premium. This service is offered by many successful companies including some of the ones mentioned in earlier chapters, such as Evernote, Cloze, and Todoist.

Job Seekers

LinkedIn stands alone in its focused quest to help professionals and jobseekers network, which is part of what fueled LinkedIn's explosive growth. It was established early on to be a safe place for companies seeking employees by separating itself from the pack, relying on business-related news and content to make up most of its online ads. Also for those who were already employed, LinkedIn became a place for people to meet. The kind of professional engagement that takes place is unlike that offered on the rest of the social media world, as users of LinkedIn tend to refrain from making brazen remarks and practice self-restraint; after all, interacting with, praising, and recommending others is offered at the expense of one's reputation and people will not pass that on as easily as they would a "like" to a funny video.

Serving a dual purpose, LinkedIn helps employers find new talent, while other job-seeking websites have lost some of their legitimacy, as employers weed through thousands of resumes each day, looking for the right candidate to fill a position. LinkedIn allows professionals to come out to speak to one another directly, and gives jobseekers the ability to show potential employers that they do indeed have valuable networking skills. Many employers now require that a LinkedIn link be included on resumes as another form of contact along with your address, phone number, and email. Remember, the hiring process costs companies time and money and by allowing them to learn more about you, LinkedIn offers them a glimpse at your professional life, and they learn about who you are in terms of your networking abilities. You will open up opportunities not just by speaking directly with others but by being sought out on the site as well.

LinkedIn recruiters can even search the LinkedIn database for potential candidates by searching for profiles with specific words in the description. It's important to make sure that your LinkedIn profile uses key words that will help employers find you, and similar to SEO, you can use words that describe you and your qualifications to help you show up when employers are searching for candidates. LinkedIn calls this "sourcing" but it acts the same way as searching for jobs on job-seeking websites. Key words will help employers find you when they're on the hunt. Not only do employers have an easy way to find their candidates, but jobseekers can also sign up to get notified whenever a job is posted.

When a potential employer finds you, they will likely look at your connections. A person with good connections would be viewed as being more desirable, especially where having good communications or good people skills come into place. Again, showing others you have a strong network says a lot about you, your work ethic and your ability to get things done. Like with any resume, or online profile, avoid garnishing your title, or making up positions to try to improve your skillset. Usually, one little white lie can send any recruiter packing, and because they have a limited amount of time and resources to work with, finding the right person involves meeting all the right requirements—including being honest—and a recruiter or employer will know right away if you're the right person. Having the right key words, a good profile and detailed information about yourself and your work history will help you stand out from the masses.

Other Online Resources

The Greatest Tool On Earth

In the greater scheme of human interaction, true networking requires meeting with people face-to-face, and establishing strong relationships with professionals and other business friends. Such relationships may later turn out to be mutually beneficial. No website or app can replace the type of bond that is formed based on seeing and feeling the reactions of others. However, that's not to say that one can't use the internet, potentially the greatest resource of our present day, to reach out to others as a way of establishing those connections. Similarly, networking skills require a person to be a good listener and to have strong communications skills, but, having good online resources, a company website or social media presence, will contribute to the growing development of your far-reaching network by offering alternative options for connecting with potential contacts. The formation of a network structure will require formed associations with various demographics, both those within your field of business and those not associated with your industry or area of expertise. Such connections may eventually offer their wisdom or help you expand from your current mind-set and into the vastness of unconventional ideas. These are the types of experiences that are possible with the right online tools. Nowadays, discovering groups within one's profession, or learning how to participate with those individuals one considers interesting, takes a little more effort than simply turning on a computer. While the internet can be very helpful, it can also be a dangerous place, particularly because of the cruelty that can arise with the level of anonymity it creates. As such, actual meetings with internet users should be approached with caution. At the same time, for those working to establish their networking skills, the anonymity associated with online social groups can inspire them to reach out, develop new relationships and set the foundation that will lead to a stronger, interconnected network.

Networking Websites for Professionals

Of all the most popular websites, many turn to Facebook, Twitter, LinkedIn and Pinterest to meet people, to promote their business, or simply for the sake of finding new job opportunities. But the best places to connect with others are sometimes hidden on lesser-known sites with a more concentrated group of users, or one with a specific niche of business-related information. Within the networking professionals group exists a growing number of websites targeted towards networking needs and providing users with new ways of expanding their business circles. Here is an overview of a few of the lesser-known but highly effective networking sites available today:

Entrepreneur

Entrepreneur (www.entrepeneur.com) is an easy-to-use website with high quality, news-related business advice, but it also concentrates on information regarding how professionals can network, communicate, and collaborate with others. It's a place for sharing business ideas and for professional networking.

Networking For Professionals (NFP)

Another great, off-the-radar website is www.networkingforprofessionals.com, which works by bringing together motivated professionals and helping them be more successful by allowing them to make the connections that are needed for enhancing their careers. On NFP, users build business contacts and even find advertisements for live events, called "NFP events", which are hosted in large cities throughout the US.

PerfectBusiness

PerfectBusiness is an online network for entrepreneurs, investors and business experts. It brings people together for the sake of promoting networking and mutual success. Also offered through their website is business-planning software, startup resources and access to a wide range of business professionals, including venture capitalists and investors. PerfectBusiness is a great tool for learning from and connecting with entrepreneurs and professionals.

Ryze

Ryze (www.ryze.com) is the bare-bones social networking website formed by Adrian Scott, Napster founding investor and advocate for social networking services. The website is a place to meet new people, share advice and find friends both new and old. Ryze also helps companies meet the right people to fit their needs. By creating a unique page with a bio and photos, one is categorized by interests, and one's talents are highlighted, allowing for a connection with those who are similar. For such a small community, it's actually a great website for anyone looking to build a platform of leads and prospects. Additionally, the overall vibe is motivational, fun and informative.

YouTube

When people think of YouTube, the first thing that comes to their minds is probably a favorite funny video. Networking might be the last thing associated with this video-sharing website, but the opportunities are actually endless. Every day, people generate billions of video views. YouTube is watched more by people 18-49 years old than is any cable network in the US, and the number of hours people spend watching YouTube videos per day is rapidly increasing.

Setting up an account is easy, and after that, all you need is a camera to get going. There are great opportunities for someone looking to attract the attention of millions of people, and a number of popular news articles are published regularly about individuals who were propelled to success and stardom with nothing more than a successful YouTube channel. What often happens is that a video goes viral (quickly generating millions of views) usually within days, and the video is then spanned across several social-media platforms, sometimes ending up getting coverage on TV. While this level of attention isn't guaranteed to everyone, it actually is the result more often than you would think. In fact, YouTube is responsible for the careers of artists such as Justin Bieber, who began his career with videos of himself singing and then suddenly became a big hit. What tends to happen when an up-and-coming artist becomes a YouTube sensation is that major producers snatch up the highly in-demand talent, and just like that, a star is born. Another example of this phenomenon is Lucas Cruikshank, who plays the YouTube personality Fred (with the "r" spelled backwards), a quirky, dysfunctional personality with a unique voice that ended up capturing the attention of millions. Fred went on to appear on the television shows *Hannah Montana* and *iCarly*, and even won a Nickelodeon Teen Choice Award. With help from his growing popularity, he became the lead in his own movie series that include *Fred: The Movie, Fred 2: Night of the Living Fred* and *Fred 3: Camp Fred.*

However, not everyone who becomes a YouTube star does it as an entertainer. Lauren Luke recently made headlines when her YouTube videos essentially made her a millionaire. She was able to turn her love for make-up into her own brand, and was successful at it. Who knew that so many people wanted advice on how to apply make-up? In the beginning, not even Lauren Luke did. It was simply a passion of hers, and by teaching young ladies new techniques they could try at home, Lauren's career took off.

Now, the message here is not to teach you to become rich and famous, but to help you realize that there is a huge potential for attracting attention through YouTube. Creating videos that others see might not make you a viral sensation, but can certainly help create networking opportunities as you draw in like-minded people who will seek to connect with you. Remember, networking is about helping others and displaying what assets you have to offer.

Beyond this, YouTube will also play a big role in helping you to establish an online presence, as people will be able to find you easily and learn more about you by watching the videos you've created. Even if you're not as zany as Fred or as make-up savvy as Lauren, by focusing on topics that spark your interest, you can potentially attract interest from other YouTubers. Imagine it: your videos are available to view by anyone, anywhere, at anytime, so it makes your online presence mainstream but also opens up opportunities outside your area, as you become exposed to a global audience. YouTube cannot make everyone rich, but it can be a great tool for building and expanding your network.

Measuring Your Success

Networking Takes Time

Building a strong network can seem like an impossible task to the novice. But those who have worked at it and relied on their ability to make connections with others know that it takes time, above all, to forge strong relationships. It can seem unnerving when your first efforts yield no results, but understand that establishing and maintaining a network of friends is a long-term investment that can create opportunities for years to come. Nonetheless, good networking requires that a person be involved with their circles, and in most cases this requires little effort but it does require making an attempt. Know when to reach out to your potential contacts, and how to conduct yourself so that you make a lasting impression. Remember to stay organized; this can help make your networking time all the more effective. A good networker can make new connections and manage their network while taking the time to meet with contacts in as little as one hour per month. Your networking success can be a difficult thing to measure, but there is one area where it's easily measurable: your online networking success.

The Net Promoter

The Net Promoter Score (https://www.netpromoter.com/) is an online resource from Net Promoter that makes surveying anyone who visits your website easy by asking one single question that can help predict various aspects of your growth. The Net Promoter Score is an index that ranges from -100 to +100 and measures an online user's willingness to recommend a website, product or service. One of the benefits of using the Net Promoter include improving a person's online experience, which can lead to greater online traffic and higher cost efficiencies, but more importantly, the Net Promoter score can help increase word-of-mouth recommendations and help you create a better product or brand.

For the small business owner, the Net Promoter can help improve a number of aspects of their business such as helping to create higher profit margins, increasing sales and improving marketing ROI. Websites that use the Net Promoter have a higher retention rate for visitors and receive increased traffic due to a greater reference through word of mouth. For someone looking to increase their online presence, the Net Promoter will improve the quality of those visiting your website through an enhanced online experience and essentially creating a greater stream of online traffic.

How Does The Net Promoter Work?

The Net Promoter metric measures satisfaction and the likelihood of whether an online user would recommend your website or service to others by asking a single question using an 10-point rating score ranging from 0 (not at all likely) to 10 (extremely likely). Based on their rating, an online user is then classified into 1 of 3 categories: promoters, passives, and, detractors.

Promoters

"Promoters" are those respondents who answer with a score of 9 or 10. These are the users who loved the website, product or service in question and they are most likely to be enthusiastic about what you are promoting, and thus have a high probability of being repeat visitors or customers and even promoting your work to others.

Passives

"Passives" are the respondents who score your survey question with a rating of 7 or 8. This category of respondents is somewhat satisfied, but they may not be someone to retain and from a business perspective, they are likely to switch products given the opportunity. Since they are not as enthusiastic about your website, service or product, chances are your passives are less likely to promote your services than your promoters would be.

Detractors

The last group, "Detractors," are those respondents who gave a score of 6 and below. The benefit to having detractors in your scoring models is that some of the best advice you can get for improving your website, product, or service is from your least satisfied visitors. However, generally speaking, detractors are not particularly interested in what you have to offer, so they are not likely to visit your website again and could potentially hurt your image with negative word of mouth.

The Net Promoter Score

Once you have evaluated a certain number of participants, you can now determine your Net Promoter Score (NPS), which is a calculation of the difference between the percentage of Promoters compared to the percentage of Detractors you surveyed. The NPS score is not a percentage but instead is measured as a number between -100 and +100. The way it works is simple: Net Promoter Score = %Promoters - %Detractors, so for example, if you have 25% Promoters, 55% Passives and 20% Detractors, your NPS score will be a +5. This may sound low, but an NPS score of 0 or greater is usually considered good by most standards.

While an NPS score can be used to measure something as simple as overall website satisfaction, many large companies use NPS as a customer feedback tool. The main goal for a large company in using NPS is to use to measure potential growth, customer satisfaction and even customer loyalty to a product, service, or to the company itself. On the Net Promoter website, the information taken from your surveys is then translated into a chart with the percentage of Detractors appearing in red, the Passives in orange, and the Promoters in green. Your NPS is then measured in a similar way, displaying a positive NPS in green, while a negative NPS appears in red. Having a way to measure the quality of your responses is important too, and while there is no way to ensure everyone is answering honestly, you can strategically set up the survey to be asked at any time during a person's visit to your website. The way the survey is asked is that it appears as a popup, and asking a user to take your survey at the end of their visit or before signing off can be helpful as the information is still fresh on their minds and the user is likely to want to take it when leaving the site, having already taken value from it, as opposed to at the beginning of their visit.

There are numerous benefits to measuring the satisfaction of those visiting your site. From large companies looking for insight about a product or service, to a networker promoting an event, listening to the views of online users can make or break a deal and the Net Promoter makes measuring online satisfaction easy. When reaching out to online users who are willing to take the time to share their thoughts with you, you can benefit directly from their concerns or ideas. Improving the experience of online visitors will not only help you appear professional, but they will genuinely enjoy visiting your website. A great benefit about taking surveys is that not only will it improve your online traffic, but you can integrate this type of data collecting to help you gain an edge if you're a small business owner looking to improve sales, marketing or customer satisfaction. A simple question, such as "How likely are you to recommend this website to others?" can help you make improvements that will improve your overall online presence.

Networking Across New Markets

Making the Most Out of Your Opportunities

In chapter 6, *Where to Start,* you learned how one of most effective ways to network was by connecting to people within the same industry as you. Networking with other like-minded individuals has the potential to unlock new career opportunities, as those you know are likely to recommend you and provide insight on jobs you may be suitable to fulfill. By having close relationships with those within your industry, you will also be kept in the loop with regards to industry news and learn about similar companies and the opportunities that may be available through them. Another great reason to start with people within your industry is that as you rely on others for help and information, you too will improve, helping you become knowledgeable and more efficient within your current position. As you develop into a more experienced worker, you can help in sharing information, a practice that helps everyone make better decisions, but also makes you someone colleagues want to come to for help. These are all great ways to establish good networking relationships with the colleagues you see most, those within your related field or industry. But what about those outside your industry circle?

Utilizing Those Outside Your Industry

For the sake of first growing your network into a robust, working circle of friends, starting with those within your industry will help open the door to new possibilities and opportunities. But a good networker is a lot like an investor in that they use diversification in order to help improve their overall results. By looking to cross over to industries outside of yours, you will open yet another vast amount of opportunities.

By relying only on people within your industry, you could reach a plateau of help and information; however, looking to new industries can uncover innovative, valuable resources. A large part of what a networking entails is getting assistance from contacts, which usually comes in the form of advice and suggestions. While your industry peers may have good advice to offer, working with people outside of your industry will encourage outside-the-box thinking and this can aid you in further developing yourself as a knowledgeable, innovative thinker. The people within your network are good for providing guidance and suggestions that can help you improve your career, but having only network contacts within your industry will limit your ability to grow, as you will experience only methods practiced within your industry.

When attending networking events, often there's a sense of competition among your peers or those within your industry, but attending events outside of your normal expectations will allow you to strategize and expand the potential of your network. Having business friends within a variety of industries will allow you to develop opportunities that would not be available otherwise.

For example, think about an architect attending a building event in his hometown where hundreds of other architects and architect firms will be attending. Sure, it might be a great place to meet others within his industry. But by making contacts outside of his normal circle of co-workers, the architect could find new opportunities by meeting a realtor, florist or even a grocery store manager who might know of a new store opening up that may require help from an architect. The realtor may have a client who wants to renovate their house, or the florist might want to build a new flower shop somewhere across town.

In any event, the people outside of the architect's field of business have created more opportunities than those within his field. Had it not been for the guidance and knowledge the architect received from his peers, he would not be the established professional he was, but by looking across new industries, the architect has opened up several great career opportunities. Look for unconventional places to expand your network, and when everyone else is attending the same events, find other events that will help you get noticed by potential contacts in industries that may need your help. Overall, making networking contacts with those outside your job field greatly improves your odds of making yourself known and will help you build relationships with influential people.

One of the best attributes you can have when networking is the ability to stand out. Networking across new markets will help you do just that, and it allows you to bring creativity and richness to new industries. Within new markets, not only will you feel like you are no longer competing for the attention of others, but you are naturally standing out and creating a demand for the value you have to offer. More so, you should make it one of your objectives to stand out, to do something great, and be a different variable within an industry which will help you create the type of uniqueness that will make a lasting impression.

There are more reasons why looking across new industries will help you develop a more robust, diverse network. In instances where you would normally be limited to a specific set of rules, or way of thinking, having people to count on from different backgrounds and perspectives helps you reach beyond the limitations of your industry. If you would normally turn to only one person for answers to a specific problem, your friends from across different sectors will help you find new ways to overcome hurdles. The same can be said when the time comes and you help people from a different industry, you will construct lasting relationships as well as develop a whole new group of exceptional resources. Diversity allows people from different walks of life to come together and find new ways of solving problems, and while you might have a great set of business friends, new perspectives can lead to greater ideas and serve as a fresh, new way to focus on either the small problems, or on issues as a whole when focusing on the big picture.

Pursing opportunities within new industries will benefit you in more ways than you'd expect. Not only will you stand out as being unique, which will help you make a lasting impression, but you're also not competing with others within your normal group of business friends for the attention of other potential contacts. Looking for networking opportunities across new markets means that you are naturally creating a demand for your brand and the value you have to offer. Further, having this elevated sense of uniqueness along with a strong brand will help create more word of mouth recommendations and even more opportunities for you.

Compare Networking Options

Within similar industries you:

- Compete for market space;
- Can been view as being the 'competition';
- There may be a low demand for you services;
- Experiences align with those of your peers.

Going into new industries:

- Create unconventional opportunities;
- There is little or no competition;
- Create or capture new demand;
- Increase your brand value;

- Find new ways of overcoming challenges.

Choosing Specific Industries

Just like choosing events as a way to help improve your chances of meeting great people to network with, choosing the industries you want to use to help diversify your network will add value to your overall networking abilities. One of the first things to do is to define which industry you wish to take the time to penetrate. It might not be the most obvious choice at first, but with some thought, attending events across new industries will help you strategize who you meet, and prepare you for what you may have to offer. As with any event, if you can find out beforehand who might be there, you can prepare yourself for who you could potentially meet, allowing you to prepare information about the person you wish to meet and the company they work for.

Based on the industry in which you're seeking new contacts, some will provide more opportunities than others. You might be a software writer who recently created a program for small businesses, and while the people in the antique trade might not be the ones to use the newest types of software available, preparing beforehand can help you make leaps and bounds over others who have tried—and failed—because you know who to contact directly. A key element to networking successfully across new markets is to know and understand the different needs of various industries. This might mean that in the automotive industry, people are more likely to joke around and want to work in a way that's quick and to the point, where those in the art industry might expect to talk to people that can offer uniqueness and richness to their product or services. As you practice communicating with others, your ability to perceive the needs of those you meet will play an important role in picking up on the needs of potential contacts from outside of your normal way of doing business.

Even if you are relatively new to networking, focus on being professional and reach out to potential business friends with the intentions of helping first. Similar to the way you can adjust your attire to meet the needs of a formal event, or something as relaxed as a baseball game, adjust your approach to meet the needs of those within the industry you wish to connect with. Should you meet someone influential who would make a great addition to your circle of business friends, but who doesn't quite meet the level of professionalism you're accustomed to, know that seeming too formal may make you appear snooty and disconnected. If this particular person has a colorful vocabulary—for example, they use the "f" word as a noun, adjective, and verb—there's no need to use such language yourself, but do your best to make sure they're comfortable speaking to you, and try not to show your discomfort at their use of language. Planning ahead might not prepare you for knowing what type of language a person might use, or whether they act in a professional manner or not, but use diversification and great communication skills to perceive and adapt to the needs of others. If all else fails, be yourself and do your best to make a lasting impression on anyone you meet.

Networking Mistakes to Avoid

Don't Make Things About 'Me'

One of the emphases of this book has been to make things about 'others' and not about yourself. This is probably one of the biggest mistakes a new networker will make. Not taking the time to get to know a new contact will almost guarantee that you will not hear from them again in the future and, should you try to make contact later when you've made little or no attempt at getting to know them first, it could also be seen as an unnatural act, or even seen as being awkward.

When you meet someone, remember not to be a passive listener. Be sure to respond, ask questions, and, most importantly, show the person that you're making an actual attempt at getting to know them by showing that you're interested in the person who's speaking. It takes practice to become a proactive listener, and while it can be hard to come up with new questions to ask each person you meet, you can save yourself some trouble by having a set of favorites that you can use when meeting just about anyone. Avoid asking closed questions, those that require a yes or no answer. "So, you like coming here?" If they didn't, then they wouldn't have bothered to show up. Learn to generate open-ended questions that require the participant to explain their answers.

When you speak, remember to remain professional and assume that you're speaking to other professionals who are also looking to make strong networking contacts. Allow others to see that you're worth getting to know, and if you're an expert or hold special knowledge of your industry or job, make sure you use that when introducing yourself using your elevator hook. Keep in mind that a controlling listener is someone who continually turns the conversation back to themselves, and this is as bad, if not worse, than being someone who says very little. Don't outdo someone. If someone caught the biggest fish ever, don't try to tell them that you caught an even bigger one, as a controlling listener might do.

After meeting so many great people, you're bound to come across some that have obvious potty mouths. These very people may be someone you're interested in networking with as they may be regarded highly within their industry. The main approach in dealing with people like this is to not speak negatively about your-self, your company or your coworkers. A person who swears a lot might not necessarily be someone negative, but if this is the case, remain positive and optimistic, and chances are your good attitude will rub off on them.

Letting Others Do The Work For You

Networking is an involved process, and having business friends in high places does not guarantee that they will be there for you when you need them. Don't assume that someone else will put in a good word for you simply because you know them. If you know there is a way for your contact to help you, sometimes you just have to ask, but don't expect much if you're not someone who has offered them help in the first place. A person you help will natu-rally want to help you, and just knowing them is not grounds for being offered great opportunities. Relying on the generosity of others will not always get you the things you want most, and in networking, it's those who make the initial steps who will benefit from others. Don't wait until you are formally introduced to someone you want to meet. Take the first step, reach out, and introduce yourself, then make the connections you need in order to get what you want out of your career. Don't wait until you need a network to start networking with others.

It's hard enough turning supervisors into networking contacts, but if you do manage to pull it off, do not simply assume they will recommend you for that new position or refer you for a project you would like to take on. One thing you can do is ask if you can be of help and show your willingness to assist colleagues, along with your enthusiasm for work. Creating opportunities means taking the time to get involved. Don't rely solely on knowing the right people to be the solution to everything. Networking is a great way to help improve your career, but meeting people and showing them they can depend on you are two separate skill sets.

Even though your business friends might be attending a great event in your area, don't assume you'll always be invited. This is why it's so important to keep in touch with them, so that you remain in the loop about events or activities that might be happening where you could meet new people and expand your network. Don't rely on others to do your networking for you; it's up to you to reach out and find out what your contacts are doing. By making an earnest attempt, your chances to become a successful networker will improve greatly.

Don't Depend Solely On Friends And Family
Friends and family are usually the first point of contact when you need help, but don't rely solely on them to make up the entirety of your networking circle. For one thing, your close friends see you differently than they see everyone else, and even your inner-circle friends with great careers might not make the same recommendations or referrals as your professional friends. While those within your larger circle of friends, as discussed in Chapter 11, will help

expand your networking possibilities, it's important to know that some of the best networking contacts you make are with people you don't know very well.

A strong network requires you to have contacts within your industry and outside your industry. Think of this when considering your personal friends as networking prospects. Having personal friends within your network is very much possible, but consider this: you spend a lot of time with your personal friends, and of this time, how much of it is spent talking about non-business-related topics? Consider whether or not you any useful professional advice actually gets exchanged when you meet your friends. You may get along great with your personal friends, but they can offer very little at keeping you in mind when opportunities arise. Facebook, LinkedIn and other websites are great for keeping in touch, but don't rely on them to help you establish the type of contacts that you can grow with in the long-term—people that can help you make the right connections, and those who will help you when needed. Advancing in your career means learning how to become great at what you do, but your network is what helps pave the path you will need to get ahead.

Don't Sell Anything

Too many people confuse networking with something it's not—having the opportunity to meet others for the sake of selling a service or product. This is a huge misconception and an approach that should never be taken when first meeting someone. Instead, tell potential business friends about what you do, but keep it brief. If a person is in need of your product or service, they will solicit what they need from you, or ask for more information in the future. Meeting someone only with the intention to have them sign up for something is the fastest way to make a potential contact not want to call you back, or follow up with you later.

Don't expect to 'get' anything right away. In most circumstances, you must give first, and focus on building a relationship before asking for any favors. A successful network execution is about giving, investing and demonstrating a willingness to help your business friends. As you will learn, at almost every networking event you attend you will likely meet someone who is working hard at making their sales pitch heard, but those people are often excluded from forming the types of relationships needed to help develop a prolonged, fruitful networking relationship. Your goal should be to meet people, make connections, and if possible, exchange contact information.

Don't Become Impatient

Networking does not happen overnight, and when it feels like your efforts are being shunned, remember that networking is a process that requires you to go out and get involved. Meeting people, joining groups and clubs, taking a few minutes to call or email your contacts are all necessary for your network to become an established, functioning system. Most of your energy should be focused on meeting new people, followed by finding avenues where you can make yourself helpful to others. Expecting too much too soon from any network is commonly misconstrued. Networking is a skill and like any other skill, it takes practice. Finding out how to put your talents to work for you will help extraordinarily, and once you find the confidence to speak to anyone anytime, you will have become a great networker, one with the ability to succeed and fulfill a higher level of professional satisfaction. Just remember that it takes time, and that all networking opportunities start with a conversation.

Just a Little Reminder

Networking is not something that happens easily, but now you have a better understanding of how meeting other people and making good impressions form the base for developing long lasting relationships. Not only is it not something taught to most people in school, networking has become something akin to those searching for admission into a secret society. While past generations had essential needs to communicate with others, in today's age, networking has taken on a different meaning and could even be seen as a lost art, as the true essence of networking had been one thing: meeting with people face to face. Trying to remember everything you need to do might seem daunting, but fear not, for here is a few points that will serve as a valuable reminder when deciding what to do to make the right connections. Take the time to look through these steps and make having the ability to network successfully, work for you.

Be prepared: there's nothing worse than getting yourself into a great networking opportunity and then blowing it because you're not prepared with questions or an elevator hook—be ready.

Be a good listener: nobody likes to talk to a brick wall—learn to listen, and people will want to talk to you.

Be different: same is boring, different is fun—don't be forgettable.

Build relationships, even if there's no obvious payoff: build as many real, long-term relationships as you can—you never know when it might come in handy.

Branch out: don't focus just on your industry—that's what everyone else is doing, and meanwhile you can be making fruitful connections with all kinds of different people.

Technology is your friend: use technology to keep your networking contacts organized, and use the internet to make yourself findable.

Be a giver, not a taker: focus first on *giving* value to someone you meet, and the relationship that follows will pay you back tenfold.

Networking is the most powerful way to grow your business and career. Face to face is always best, but use every tool at your disposal. Treat your contacts like friends and watch your network—and your career—grow. Be brave. Get out there. Get connected.

Networking Is A Valuable Skill

Until the last decade or so, networking had been seen as a commodity, but not as something that was necessary in order to succeed. Today, networking is becoming a necessary skill needed in order to get ahead. Connecting with the right people has the potential to advance careers and create opportunities, but because it's not something to offer immediate rewards, many tend to disregard its potential.

Most importantly, networking is about building relationships and you should treat the people within your network as friends, and not as mere contacts. Do for others first and your rewards will come with time. You have what it takes to go out there and meet new people. Don't be afraid—you never know where the unexpected might take you.

About The Author

Eleazar Anthony Noel is the Founder and Managing Director of Roots and Culture Magazine founded in 2007. Noel has also worked with magazines such as Beautiful Barbuda Magazine, Food and Drinks Magazines, and Small Business Entrepreneur Magazines, just to name a few. Additionally, Noel is the Founder of ELE Training and Consultancy Services and the Vice President of Business Development and Marketing at Ibusol – Invaluable Business Solution.

Noel has been doing business since the age of 18. He has worked with businesses throughout the Caribbean, United States, United Kingdom, Italy, Venezuela, Columbia and Ethiopia. Noel believes in giving back. In 2008, Noel formed the Eleazar Anthony Noel Foundation, which aims to assist with the social development of young people. He also founded the ELE Project, a mentoring program for young, aspiring entrepreneurs.

Noel is an award winning Entrepreneurship Facilitator, Lecturer, and currently holds a Graduate Diploma in Management and a Masters in Business Administration majoring in Marketing from the Australian Institute of Business. He is currently pursuing doctoral studies for a Doctor of Business Administration with Heriot-Watt University, Edinburgh Business School. Noel is indeed an entrepreneur, philanthropist, activist, author, and public speaker.

Founded in 2010 by Eleazar Anthony Noel, The ELE Project was formed with a desire to bring aspiring entrepreneurs closer together. Noel, being a young entrepreneur, saw it necessary to create a platform where budding entrepreneurs can have an opportunity to exchange ideas and views, inspire each other, seek expert advice and learn and grow through the many networking opportunities.

The ELE Project seeks to provide the tools and resources to empower young promising entrepreneurs to realize their dreams and make a contribution to a better world.

Our mission is to inspire and grow new ideas through transparency and collaboration. No matter where you are starting, or where you are going, The ELE Project creates a community that allows budding entrepreneurs to learn, track their progress and grow.

WHAT PARTICIPANTS OF THE ELE PROJECT ARE SAYING:

I have learned so much from the gathering. I really enjoy getting the opportunity to meet with successful entrepreneurs from around the world who not only inspired me to move forward with my ideas but also assisted me in developing new ideas. This program has opened so many doors for me. My future as an entrepreneur is brighter because of The ELE Project. – **Sandy Smith**

The ELE Project has opened my eyes to the world of business and entrepreneurship. Being a young person, I can safely say that the exposure and insight provided by this project, has hugely benefited me. I'd certainly recommend this to anyone who may need that push in the right direction or seeking the advice of any other successful businessmen or women - **Michael Charles**

Contact Eleazar

Website: www.eleazarnoel.com
Email: info@eleazarnoel.com
Facebook: Eleazar Anthony Noel
LinkedIn: Eleazar Noel
YouTube: ELE – Educate Lead Encourage
Twitter: @ele_noel

www.ingramcontent.com/pod-product-compliance
Lightning Source LLC
Chambersburg PA
CBHW022010170526
45157CB00003B/1220